rainbow
GOD

the seven colors of love

johnny & elizabeth
ENLOW

rainbow
GOD

the seven colors of love

johnny & elizabeth
ENLOW

This book is dedicated to our lineage.
May we honor those we love who have gone before us
and those who will come after us
with the ways we have discovered and communicated the God
we have come to know.
May our children and their children know the real Him
in ever-increasing ways,
until the truth of how good He is floods the whole earth.

RAINBOW GOD
THE SEVEN COLORS OF LOVE

Dear Reader,

We'd like to share a few helpful things with you to keep in mind as you are reading.

1. It's highly likely that you've never read a book written by a husband and wife quite like this one. Just like any husband and wife, we see things and express what we see differently. It is our hope that as you read, you will not be distracted by the back and forth style of our communication or worry too much over who is saying what, but that you would experience our thoughts as a seamless teaching and dialogue on the vast subject of God. In order to bring some differentiation, we have put a simple strategy in place. **Johnny's words are typed in a regular font and Elizabeth's words are italicized.**

2. Our goal in writing this book was simple: to expand the reader's perspective of who they think God is. If you are not open and hungry spiritually to learn more about God, then you may not get much out of this book and we apologize in advance.

3. If you are finding yourself at a time in life where you want to understand new things about yourself and God, then get ready to go on a thought provoking journey where you are sure to have genuine encounters with God throughout the pages of this book.

4. We consider ourselves to be Christians who are spiritual, but not religious (which we will explain later in the book). Because we don't want the book to feel religious, rather than put scripture references in our dialogue, we have put them in footnotes. We have also used footnotes to go into a little more depth on subjects that only a few may really be interested in.

5. Some of you may prefer to read a book with more stories and less teaching than this one. If it is more difficult for you to pay attention, you may consider reading only a few pages a day, in order to break it up and be able to better absorb it. Because our desire is to present what may become a fresh perspective and a new mentality about God, we attempted to be repetitive in order to help learners of all types. Remember that repetition is required in order for us to really own a concept as our personal conviction. Read all the way through—you'll be glad you did!

6. There are several times in the book where we encourage you as the reader to put the book down and process something in a more personal way with God. That may sound a bit silly, but we encourage you to approach this book as a potentially life changing encounter with God. So look out for those opportunities and consider taking the challenge in the moment. Who knows, it might just lead you to having a story of your own to tell!

7. Pay close attention to the subtitles in each chapter as you read. They aren't just there to break up the pages into smaller sections, but are a helpful guide to an overall format we are using throughout the entire book. The subtitles will navigate you through an intentional template in gaining a fresh view of yourself and of God.

8. If you want to get the most out of this, then read it slowly and plan on taking awhile to go through it. It will actually shift you into a new mentality not only about God, but about every area of life, which takes time and thoughtful personal processing. There are a couple of ways you can read the book: the usual way, one chapter at a time, or in segments as a 90 day devotional. You would simply read the intro and then one subtitled section a day.

9. At the back of the book you will find a Quick Reference Chart that simplifies the overall template of each aspect of God as Love and how His love is displayed in each area of culture. We included it

knowing that it will especially mean something to you by the end of the book.

However you ended up with this book in your hands, we pray God Himself—nothing less and nothing more—will meet with you in just the way that you can receive it. Above all else, may you gain an increased perspective of How good He is and how much He loves you. Thank you for taking your time to read this book. We are truly honored to have the opportunity to speak into this season of your relationship with your God.

Johnny and Elizabeth

Introduction—Questions That Must Be Answered

GOD. no Matter what you were taught, or not taught about who or what He is, we all have questions about Him.

Who is He? What is He? If He exists, is He good? Should He be trusted? How involved is He in my life? And if He is involved, what in the world is He thinking? Where was He when...? Where is He now? Does He care about me? Does He really care about all the suffering in the world?

Do I matter? Am I important? Is surviving this life all there is? Will I ever feel truly loved? Will I ever feel something other than pain, emptiness, and loneliness?

No matter what your official religion or belief status is, how you answer these questions is, in fact, the most important thing about **you.**[1] Even if you believe there is no God, it is still the most important thing about you. Who you become and what your life produces will be directly connected to your perspective of God. If you have seen Him as less powerful than He is, it will have a great affect on you. If you have seen Him to be less good than He really is, it will greatly affect you. If you have seen Him to be less relevant to life than He really is, then the adverse effects on your life will be equally as profound.

What if the whole point of life is to discover the answers to these questions? Are you willing to take the risk of disappointment and fear of dealing with the pain that is behind the hard questions? Although we were both raised in Christian families and grew up in Christian churches, we went through enough heartache in life to begin asking those hard questions early on. Pain

---

1   One of A.W. Tozer's best-known quotes is: "What comes into our minds when we think about God is the most important thing about us." From *The Knowledge of the Holy,* p. 1, ©1961 by A.W. Tozer, Harper SanFrancisco.

has a way of doing that to you—either forcing the issue to the surface or burying it deep enough to ignore.

Are you ready to explore a God who is so much more than most of us have imagined or been told that it jolts you into a new way of experiencing life? Our perspectives of who God is and what He is like are most often formulated by our upbringing and then our reaction to our upbringing. If our childhood left us with happy memories, along with instruction about who God is, then we generally are able to hold on to perspectives of a good God and continue to live out a relationship with Him. On the other hand, if our early experiences in life were fraught with trauma and family fractures, we often find our beliefs about God have deteriorated. We see Him as either nonexistent or someone who can't be trusted. There are obviously innumerable perspectives on who God is and what He is like, but the one that matters most is **yours.**

In recent years, much deserved attention has come to our need to find the reason we are here, our purpose. Pastor Rick Warren's excellent book *The Purpose Driven Life* has been widely received and read by many who are not Christians. It has helped our generation deal with questions like, "What am I here for? What is my purpose and how do I fulfill it?" Ultimately everyone wants to know their purpose in life. Our personal journeys have brought us to the realization that we were made by God and for Him. We have also realized that even though settling these questions of our purpose are vital for a meaningful existence, the answers cannot be discovered or understood without an expanded perspective of who God is.

An expanded perspective of God becomes a life changer for anyone who has experienced it. Though we don't by any means claim to have a full perspective of God ourselves, we do claim to have grown greatly in our own personal perceptions of who He is. This growth has been revolutionary in our own lives, as well as for those we have the privilege of interacting with. For us, every time our individual perspectives of God have expanded, it has resulted in drastic changes in our quality of life and a greater understanding of our purpose in life, individually and as a couple.

The God each of us sees is the God we show others. As your view of Him expands, you then give others the opportunity to see God in new ways. You could show someone else the expanded view of God that you wish you had been introduced to.

I grew up in as wonderful a home as any I have heard of. My parents were God-loving people who served the Lord as pastors and missionaries. God was the priority of our household and of the way we lived. The church movement we were a part of was radical in its expression and devotion to God. We were taught that God was to be prioritized in every way possible, and not just on Sunday mornings. He was to be prioritized in how we dressed, in how we interacted with the opposite sex, in how intensely we sang in worship in the multiple church services we had to attend every week. He was to be thought of in every word we spoke and in every attitude we expressed. God was everywhere at all times, and He could see and hear everything we were doing. Therefore it behooved us to not do or say anything that might displease Him.

Though I brought many acceptable perspectives of God into my adulthood, there were also many unacceptable ones that came from my childhood—perspectives that I no longer carry and that have changed my life because what I think about God is the most important thing about *me*. The God I grew up with was a good God—theoretically. But in reality, He seemed also pretty much a stern principal who was always looking over my shoulder, ready to chide me for any ungodly action, thought, or deed. The God I grew up with did not love most things about this world or this life. He despised sports and entertainment because they kept stealing people's attention from Himself. The fact that boys would notice pretty girls was tremendously distasteful to Him, and definitely not holy. The God I knew cared very little for anything here on earth, including the earth itself. It would all burn up one day, and that day could be any day now.

The God I grew up with couldn't care less whether the planet was contaminated or not. He did not like the fact that girls played with dolls and dressed up. He was annoyed by boys and all of their rambunctiousness. My family's God thought children did not need toys or entertainment of any sort. He was decidedly serious. Anything that was not about going to church or reading the Bible or praying was just so beneath Him that He could barely stand it. I grew up perceiving that the only time I was really pleasing Him was when I was in church. Furthermore, that was really the only subject we could even talk about. God did not like to talk about anything that was not religious. I loved playing soccer, but didn't dare talk to Him about that. I mainly just hoped He could ignore me and tolerate it while I played and thought about soccer. I had friends, passions, and desires, but they were not to be brought to God. My "growing up God" was pretty much a one-tone, one-color, single-interest God who loved me—but barely, because I was so darn human, earthly, and distracted by "earthly" things.

We have had the privilege of traveling all over the world and of being exposed to multiple cultures. In much the same way that the culture of our childhood homes contributes to the way we perceive God, we have observed that every nation's culture also has a tremendous influence on how God is perceived by people of that nation. Every culture, or way of "doing" life, whether individually or as societies, contributes to the perception (usually a distortion) of who God is.

By and large, the trend seems to be the projection of a God who is very limited in His ability to identify with us—a God who is very stiff, uncreative, rigid, boring, demanding, religious, and ultimately hard to interact with. These perceptions lead us to a host of questions regarding His power and goodness. If He is so powerful and so good, just why are we in such a mess? Why are there millions of AIDS orphans? Why are there so many starving? Why are there so many in forced sexual slavery? Why is there so much violence, sickness, and death? Everything seems to suggest a God who either doesn't exist, or worse, isn't good. If He exists and is good, surely His world would not be so out of control.

If we have not wrestled with and answered these questions correctly, we bring to our cultures solutions born in the hearts of those with orphan mentalities. We solve the world's problems the best we can from our wounded hearts and ways, which will never be God's heart for us. When we live from hearts that deep down feel abandoned by God, we will only produce a culture in our homes and in our nations that reflects the God we see. We will only properly care about what we think He cares about. And whatever we think He doesn't care about, we will either not care about it ourselves or will respond to it driven by our collective fears and wounds. As they say, "How's that working for us?!"

Think about this on a personal level. Whether your parents ever talked to you about God or not, what parallels do you see in things you believed or currently believe about God that are similar to your childhood? If your parents weren't around or never spoke of Him, perhaps you tend to see God as distant, at best. If your parents or authority figures seemed overwhelmed by you or especially worried about how you would turn out, maybe you interact with a God who thinks your life is so complicated He couldn't possibly help until you get it together first. Maybe He is disappointed with you, and the choices you have made have left this God of yours looking at you through eyes of disgust and shame. Maybe your God is loving but uninvolved in the details of your life because He has more important things to take care of, so you beg Him to occasionally get involved. Perhaps you struggle in a never-ending cycle of either trying to fix your life or wanting to quit and stay as "medicated" from your pain as possible. When you have extra energy, do you look for someone else to blame or heap it on yourself? If you can identify with any of this, then you need a healed and expanded view of God.[2] It can change everything.

It changed everything for us. Our expanded perspective of God has not gone unchallenged by the realities of life and crisis. However,

---

2 Several years ago we began a friendship with Bob Hartley, founder of Deeper Waters Ministry. It is important that we acknowledge that he introduced us to this new mentality and language of a "healed and expanded view of God" and we highly recommend his resources on the subject of hope. Check out his website at www.BobHartley.org.

we have grown to have an unwavering perspective of who we have seen Him to be—better than we ever hoped. This expanded perspective of who He is has allowed us to live life like we never lived before, free to love and be loved by a Father who cares far more than we thought—about us and about the details of life. God was the one-tone, one-color God. We have since come to know Him as the Rainbow God.

Before, He was the One who loved us, but mainly as it related to us getting to heaven one day. But we now see Him as the God of all of life, the many colors of love. We see Him everywhere and in everything, quick to offer His compassionate heart and perfect solutions for the problems around us. He not only cares, but is passionate about all areas of life and of culture because it all originated in Him and is the essence of who He is.

Family. Religion. Government. Media. Education. Economy. Art and Entertainment. What are you interested in? What do you care about? What is it that you see about our culture that makes you passionate to the point of giving your life or career to it, or a frustration that makes you angry enough to want to change it and make a difference? What if that thing in you is God? What if He does care after all, through you? What if the very thing that has captured your attention since you were little—that thing that you wish you had the money or courage or talent to do the rest of your life—is there because God put it in you? What if that thing that you are good at is Him? What if He isn't hidden in the walls of a cathedral or dead behind the religious rituals human beings have settled for? The proof that God cares about politics, a stable income, and a good movie is the fact that you care. Could He be closer to you than you perceived, felt, or were told? Could He possibly be more real, relevant, and better than you have thought?

It is our hope that as you bring your questions with you through the pages of this book, you will gain a healed and expanded view of God that will cause you to live like never before.

CHAPTER ONE

Rainbow God

I (Johnny) have always been fascinated by rainbows. They give us a sense of viewing something mystical and almost supernatural. How do these seven colors just show up in the sky? Yes, I know the science behind it; it's because of the prism effect brought on by the presence of rain and sunlight. But it's still amazing and awe-inspiring. When I was little I wondered why you can never actually find the end of a rainbow. How does it seemingly stay just out of reach? And why do the specific seven colors show up? Why not just three colors or twenty? Science has a clear explanation for the process that causes them. Assuming God created the process by which they appear and we see them, I like to consider what the rainbow tells us about God.

Maybe, like me, you were taught and believe the Biblical account of the first rainbow appearing after the great flood. God spoke to Noah and said it would be a sign that He would never destroy the world again—like He had just done. What an encouraging and important promise for those who may be tempted to believe end of the world scenarios that we often hear about.

Or maybe you don't believe that the Bible and its stories are real or literally true. But consider this: even among those who are not Christians, the rainbow is generally first associated with the story of Noah's ark and the great flood. Why? Perhaps it's because there is no event mentioned in the Bible that has more historical corroborations than the flood in Genesis that destroyed almost all life on planet earth. The Koran, Greeks, Babylonians, Mayas, and over 500 other cultures report, as part of their known history, a period when there was a great flood of mass destruction. There are definite similarities to the stories that have been communicated from one generation to the next. Most accounts include a catastrophic flood where only one family was saved in an ark or large boat and the release of some kind of bird sent out to search for proof of dry land after seven days (details that are all in the original Biblical text). These great flood traditions have been passed down in China, Iraq, Wales, Russia, India, America, Hawaii, Peru, Sumatra, Scandinavia, and Polynesia—to name just a few of the very diverse locations. The stories contain such unusual similarities that if any story from the Bible seems safe to believe, it's the one that brought us the first mention of the rainbow.

NOAH'S ARK

The Message[1] version of the Bible tells the story like this: (You can skip this part if you are already familiar with the story.)

"When the human race began to increase, with more and more daughters being born, the sons of God noticed that the daughters of men were beautiful. They looked them over and picked out wives for themselves.

---

1 If you are unfamiliar with different versions of the Bible, *The Message* translation is a great one to start with because it is written in everyday language rather than the "thees" and "thous" of the King James Version that was translated back in the early 1600s.

"Then God said, "I'm not going to breathe life into men and women endlessly. Eventually they're going to die; from now on they can expect a life span of 120 years."

"This was back in the days (and also later) when there were giants in the land. The giants[2] came from the union of the sons of God and the daughters of men. These were the mighty men of ancient lore, the famous ones.

"God saw that human evil was out of control. People thought evil, imagined evil—evil, evil, evil from morning to night. God was sorry that he had made the human race in the first place; it broke his heart. God said, "I'll get rid of my ruined creation, make a clean sweep: people, animals, snakes and bugs, birds—the works. I'm sorry I made them."

"But Noah was different. God liked what he saw in Noah.

"This is the story of Noah: Noah was a good man, a man of integrity in his community. Noah walked with God. Noah had three sons: Shem, Ham, and Japheth. As far as God was concerned, the Earth had become a sewer; there was violence everywhere. God took one look and saw how bad it was, everyone corrupt and corrupting—life itself corrupt to the core.

"God said to Noah, "It's all over. It's the end of the human race. The violence is everywhere; I'm making a clean sweep. Build yourself a ship from teakwood. Make rooms in it. Coat it with pitch inside and out. Make it 450 feet long, seventy-five feet wide, and forty-five feet high. Build a roof for it and put in a window eighteen inches from the top; put in a door on the side of the ship; and make three decks, lower, middle, and upper. I'm going to bring a flood on the Earth that will destroy

2   Giants?! Yes, the Bible speaks of giants, or Nephilim, as beings who were the offspring of fallen angels and humans that lived on the earth. The Bible and other historical writings speak of them as having unusual supernatural strength and skills that somehow contributed to the prevailing evil of that generation. Evidently it was so bad that God regretted even creating humanity.

everything alive under Heaven. Total destruction. But I'm going to establish a covenant with you: You'll board the ship, and your sons, your wife and your sons' wives will come on board with you. You are also to take two of each living creature, a male and a female, on board the ship, to preserve their lives with you: two of every species of bird, mammal, and reptile—two of everything so as to preserve their lives along with yours. Also get all the food you'll need and store it up for you and them."

"Noah did everything God commanded him to do.

"Next God said to Noah, "Now board the ship, you and all your family—out of everyone in this generation, you're the righteous one. Take on board with you seven pairs of every clean animal, a male and a female; one pair of every unclean animal, a male and a female; and seven pairs of every kind of bird, a male and a female, to insure their survival on Earth. In just seven days I will dump rain on Earth for forty days and forty nights. I'll make a clean sweep of everything that I've made."

"Noah did everything God commanded him. Noah was 600 years old when the floodwaters covered the Earth. Noah and his wife and sons and their wives boarded the ship to escape the flood. Clean and unclean animals, birds, and all the crawling creatures came in pairs to Noah and to the ship, male and female, just as God had commanded Noah. In seven days the floodwaters came. It was the six-hundredth year of Noah's life, in the second month, on the seventeenth day of the month that it happened: all the underground springs erupted and all the windows of Heaven were thrown open. Rain poured for forty days and forty nights.

"That's the day Noah and his sons Shem, Ham, and Japheth, accompanied by his wife and his sons' wives, boarded the ship.

And with them every kind of wild and domestic animal, right down to all the kinds of creatures that crawl and all kinds of birds and anything that flies. They came to Noah and to the ship in pairs—everything and anything that had the breath of life in it, male and female of every creature came just as God had commanded Noah. Then God shut the door behind him.

"The flood continued forty days and the waters rose and lifted the ship high over the Earth. The waters kept rising, the flood deepened on the Earth, the ship floated on the surface. The flood got worse until all the highest mountains were covered—the high-water mark reached twenty feet above the crest of the mountains. Everything died. Anything that moved—dead. Birds, farm animals, wild animals, the entire teeming exuberance of life—dead. And all people—dead. Every living, breathing creature that lived on dry land died; he wiped out the whole works—people and animals, crawling creatures and flying birds, every last one of them, gone. Only Noah and his company on the ship lived. The floodwaters took over for 150 days.

"Then God turned his attention to Noah and all the wild animals and farm animals with him on the ship. God caused the wind to blow and the floodwaters began to go down. The underground springs were shut off, the windows of Heaven closed and the rain quit. Inch by inch the water lowered. After 150 days the worst was over.

"On the seventeenth day of the seventh month, the ship landed on the Ararat mountain range. The water kept going down until the tenth month. On the first day of the tenth month the tops of the mountains came into view. After forty days Noah opened the window that he had built into the ship. He sent out a raven; it flew back and forth waiting for the floodwaters to dry up. Then he sent a dove to check on the flood conditions, but it couldn't even find a place to perch—water still covered the Earth. Noah reached out and caught it, brought it back into the ship.

"He waited seven more days and sent out the dove again. It came back in the evening with a freshly picked olive leaf in its beak. Noah knew that the flood was about finished.

"He waited another seven days and sent the dove out a third time. This time it didn't come back.

"In the six-hundred-first year of Noah's life, on the first day of the first month, the flood had dried up. Noah opened the hatch of the ship and saw dry ground. By the twenty-seventh day of the second month, the Earth was completely dry.

"God spoke to Noah: "Leave the ship, you and your wife and your sons and your sons' wives. And take all the animals with you, the whole menagerie of birds and mammals and crawling creatures, all that brimming prodigality of life, so they can reproduce and flourish on the Earth."

"Noah disembarked with his sons and wife and his sons' wives. Then all the animals, crawling creatures, birds—every creature on the face of the Earth—left the ship family by family. Noah built an altar to God. He selected clean animals and birds from every species and offered them as burnt offerings on the altar.

"God smelled the sweet fragrance and thought to himself, "I'll never again curse the ground because of people. I know they have this bent toward evil from an early age, but I'll never again kill off everything living as I've just done. For as long as Earth lasts, planting and harvest, cold and heat, summer and winter, day and night will never stop."

"God blessed Noah and his sons: He said, "Prosper! Reproduce! Fill the Earth! Every living creature—birds, animals, fish—will fall under your spell and be afraid of you. You're responsible for them. All living creatures are yours for food;

just as I gave you the plants, now I give you everything else. Except for meat with its lifeblood still in it—don't eat that. But your own lifeblood I will avenge; I will avenge it against both animals and other humans. Whoever sheds human blood, by humans let his blood be shed, because God made humans in his image reflecting God's very nature. You're here to bear fruit, reproduce, lavish life on the Earth, live bountifully!"

"Then God spoke to Noah and his sons: "I'm setting up my covenant with you including your children who will come after you, along with everything alive around you—birds, farm animals, wild animals—that came out of the ship with you. I'm setting up my covenant with you that never again will everything living be destroyed by floodwaters; no, never again will a flood destroy the Earth."

"God continued, "This is the sign of the covenant I am making between me and you and everything living around you and everyone living after you. I'm putting my rainbow in the clouds, a sign of the covenant between me and the Earth. From now on, when I form a cloud over the Earth and the rainbow appears in the cloud, I'll remember my covenant between me and you and everything living, that never again will floodwaters destroy all life. When the rainbow appears in the cloud, I'll see it and remember the eternal covenant between God and everything living, every last living creature on Earth."

"And God said, "This is the sign of the covenant that I've set up between me and everything living on the Earth."

"The sons of Noah who came out of the ship were Shem, Ham, and Japheth. Ham was the father of Canaan. These are the three sons of Noah; from these three the whole Earth was populated."[3]

---

3 Genesis 6:5–9:19, *The Message: the Bible in contemporary language,* by Eugene Peterson. Colorado Springs, Colo.: NavPress, 2002.

THE PROMISE

So the earth had been covered with floodwaters, and all had died because of their extremely evil ways—except for Noah and his family. It seems even demons, also known as fallen angels, had mixed into the human race and so much so, that possibly all were corrupted except for Noah and his family. God then instructed Noah to be fruitful and multiply and to increase upon the earth. God speaks of His new covenant with Noah and his family and with all the living animals that Noah had with them. This new promise of the preservation of creation was not just with the humans on the ark but with every living creature on the ark.

This insight alone has expanded my childhood view of God. I had seen Him as a God who cared only for humans. But here He is making a covenant with animals and every living thing. The New International Version of the Bible states the essence of the new covenant, or promise, like this:

> "Never again will I curse the ground because of humans, even though every inclination of the human heart is evil from childhood. And never again will I destroy all living creatures, as I have done. As long as the earth endures, seedtime and harvest, cold and heat, summer and winter, day and night will never cease." [4]

> "I will establish my covenant with you: Never again will all life be cut off by the waters of a flood; never again will there be a flood to destroy the earth." [5]

Many tinker with this covenant and state that God was only promising to not destroy the world specifically with a flood. In fact, it is widely believed by many Christians that God will come and

---

[4] Genesis 8:21-22, New International Version
[5] Genesis 9:11, New International Version

destroy the world again because of sin and evil on the earth. There seems to be a lack of understanding of some scriptures relating to the end times, especially 2 Peter 3:3-13. Many believe that the end of all things will be a repeat destruction (or worse) of the planet. This subject deserves an in depth study. I won't attempt to explain here, but an article is available on our website that is provided at the end of this book for those interested.

If we believe that the world is destined to be destroyed, then this covenant and the meaning of the rainbow hold very little real value. What comfort is it supposed to bring humanity that, though we won't be judged by a catastrophic flood, we will still be judged and destroyed by some other means? That's about as much comfort as being promised execution by a firing squad rather than the gallows. If it's still execution, it really doesn't matter that much.

When God said, "Never again will I destroy all living creatures," He is not trying to be sneaky with technicalities by saying, "I am never going to destroy you with a flood, but I will find another way." That's the perspective of God that needs to be healed in many of us. The fact that we could believe in a God who would be deceptive in this way says a lot about *us*, not Him. God has already prefaced His statement with "even though every inclination of his heart is evil from childhood." He already had counted on the reality that man would provoke Him to again rid the earth of their evil. It's as if God was saying, "I know you are going to tend towards evil, but even if it gets as bad as this generation again, I will not resort to total destruction." Not only that, He is also saying that as long as the earth endures, we will continue to have seasons and days and nights. This promise should address some of our fears of a meteor hitting earth, thus throwing us into total darkness or off of our seasonal rotations. God has promised that He will never totally destroy humanity with judgments and never allow the earth to be thrown into the chaos of living without the cycle of seasons and days and nights.

God described this promise in great detail, explaining who the covenant was with and what would represent it:

> "This is the sign of the covenant I am making between me and you and every living creature with you, a covenant for all generations to come: I have set my rainbow in the clouds, and it will be the sign of the covenant between me and the earth. Whenever I bring clouds over the earth and the rainbow appears in the clouds, I will remember my covenant between me and you and all living creatures of every kind. Never again will the waters become a flood to destroy all life. Whenever the rainbow appears in the clouds, I will see it and remember the everlasting covenant between God and all living creatures of every kind on the earth.
>
> "So God said to Noah, "This is the sign of the covenant I have established between me and all life on the earth."[6]

If we are going to get clarity on what the rainbow tells us about God, then we have to get the full effect of what the rainbow represents. The covenant is between God, human beings, and every living creature. So though God did give us permission to eat animals as needed,[7] He still loves and cares for animals. He loves them differently than He loves us—we're made in His image, and animals aren't—but He loves them as His creation.

God states His heartfelt promise as thoroughly as possible and seems to expand His parameters of mercy even as He is speaking. He ends up telling Noah that this is a covenant with *all life*. God has a love for everything on earth that has life. We should know that as truth, even from the very first chapter of the Bible because it says that everything God created He followed with "Wow, that's really good!" (Okay, I added the wow!)

---

6   Genesis 9:12-17
7   Genesis 9:3

THE RAINBOW

In a world filled with generation after generation of religious people who proclaim a judgmental God, it's time we grow in our knowledge of the God of mercy, kindness, and forgiveness—the God who wants to love us back to life. Though familiar with the story of Noah's ark all of my life, only recently have I begun to understand the connection of the mercy of God with the rainbow. When God said that He will remember the everlasting covenant He made with us when He sees the rainbow, what is it about the rainbow that motivates Him to forgive evil and extend mercy to His creation?

The Bible describes the throne of God as having a rainbow around it. [8] Isn't it interesting that God would choose, as a reminder of His mercy, that which encircles His throne in heaven? The innermost courts of heaven are surrounded with the visual reminder of the full faceted nature of who our God is, with His heart of mercy and compassion. When God sees a rainbow, He is looking at a representation of who He is.

Think about this: when God put the law of nature into motion, establishing that every time drops of moisture in the atmosphere reflect the sun a rainbow would appear, He was planning to make an ongoing display of His true heart for us. This is evidently so significant to Him that it exists in heaven around His seat of authority, as well as on earth. So what do the colors mean—red, orange, yellow, green, blue, indigo, and violet? Why choose a rainbow to represent Himself and His covenant?

A rainbow, in essence, is just white light, even as God is Light.[9] The prism effect that happens between water and sunlight causes white light to be made visible as the seven colors of the rainbow. Of these seven colors, three can be considered the colors of the Trinity. Like the rainbow that is in actuality white light, God is one God. Yet He is

---

8   Revelation 4:3
9   1 John 1:5

also our Father, Jesus the Son of God, and the Holy Spirit. Christians refer to this 3-in-1 aspect of God as the Trinity, which literally means a group of three. These three "Trinity colors" are what some refer to as the three primary colors, which are the colors of fire, reflecting the Bible's description of God as a Consuming Fire.[10] Yellow speaks of our Father God as the Sun that shines over us all. Red speaks of Jesus and the blood that He shed on the cross that all might be free from the ravaging effects of sin that separate us from God who loves us. Blue speaks of the Holy Spirit, who is the Spirit of Truth and the aspect of God that guides and comforts us and gives us a healthy sense of conviction when we do something that is hurtful to us or others.[11]

The Bible tells us that Adam and Eve, and therefore all of us, were made in God's image.

"He said, "Let us make man in our image, in our likeness." [12]

"So God created man in His own image, in the image of God he created him; male and female He created them." [13]

It's significant that God did not say, "Let ME make man in MY image," but rather, "Let US make man in OUR image." God clearly identifies Himself as a manifold reality. This can sound very strange to us, but the truth is, we are like that ourselves. We are spirit (that part of us that will live forever), soul (our mind, will, and emotions), and a physical body (that will one day die). Not only does this obviously refer to God as the Trinity, but I believe it also confirms the seven spirits of God that are mentioned several times in the Bible.[14] Revelation explains that there are "seven spirits of God" that are before the throne of God as "seven blazing lamps." Imagine His throne room with a rainbow of seven colors and seven spirits of God that are like blazing

---

10 Deuteronomy 4:24
11 John 15:26
12 Genesis 1:26
13 Genesis 1:27
14 Revelation 1:4, 3:1, 4:5, 5:6

fires surrounding the throne. A spirit is that part of us, or part of God, that is the real essence of who we are—what makes us *us*. In the same way that you and I are much more than three parts—body, soul, and spirit—so is God much more than the Trinity. We are not simply what we do in life. A singer, for example, has more to her than her voice. She may also be a wife, a mother, and a good friend. In the same way, there are many aspects or facets of who God is. The innermost courts of heaven are surrounded with the visual reminder of the full-faceted nature of who our God is. He is One, yet Seven. He is the Light of the world that offers salvation to our eternal souls, but He is also the God of all present life—and all areas of culture.

So when God said He set the rainbow in the sky to remind Himself of His promise to us, those seven colors remind Him of the seven primary aspects of who He is. The seven colors are seven facets of His face that, when all seen together, reveal the expanded perspective of God—seven divinely coordinated dynamics of Himself that reveal the fullness of who He is.

THE FULL SPECTRUM GOD

In the early 1700s, Sir Isaac Newton discovered and published extraordinary findings about color and light: the way color is displayed in its full spectrum in a rainbow, the connection between colors and musical notes, and how each color affects us differently and therefore carries different meaning.[15] A century later, Johann Wolfgang Goethe began studying the psychological effects of colors. For instance, his experiments proved that blue gives a feeling of coolness and yellow has a warming effect. Goethe created a color wheel showing the psychological effect of each color.[16] Clearly color is significant in terms of what it represents and how it is used, especially in this age of technology and marketing, and I believe the understanding of that originated from God Himself.

15 Neil Hutchison, 2011 www.home.vicnet.net.au/
16 www.color-wheel-pro.com

Let's look at the seven colors of the rainbow as specific representations of God. We will get more specific about these nuances of who God is and why we chose which color we did to represent the different aspects of Him, but for now consider this:

BLUE displays Him as **God the Redeemer**, who we honor and worship for His wonderful plan of redemption, through Jesus, that we Christians have primarily focused on. But that is certainly not all there is to our God.

In VIOLET/PURPLE, we see Him as **God the King** who knows how to govern and rule in Heaven as well as on earth.

Through the color GREEN, we see Him as **God the Provider** who enjoys providing for His children here on earth even as He still provides for all in Heaven.

In INDIGO/DEEP BLUE, we see Him as **God the Wise Teacher** who educates us in the knowledge of all that is Him.

YELLOW shows Him as **God the Creator** who loves Arts and Entertainment.

Through ORANGE we see Him as **Papa God**, the family man.

In RED we see Him as **God the Communicator**, always speaking truth from a hopeful and redemptive perspective, as one who loves good news and inspirational reports.

Our hope is that as you continue reading, you will begin to see Him no longer as just a one-color God who ultimately only cares for your soul, but as the full spectrum God of all life who cares about everything that affects His creation. One who, even in the colors themselves, gives us insight into who He is, what He is doing, and how He thinks and operates. One who doesn't just love us from afar, but cares deeply about all that concerns us. One who will redeem our souls and also the culture around us until it reflects His true heart for us.

Speaking of culture, notice how all seven colors, or aspects of who God is, connect to the **seven main areas of culture of every nation**.[17] (We will sometimes refer to them as structures, sectors, spheres, or mountains.) They are **Family** (orange), **Religion** (blue), **Government** (violet), **Media** (red), **Education** (indigo), **Economy/ Business** (green), and **Arts/Entertainment/Sports** (yellow). These are not just the seven head structures of society upon which all nations are built; these are seven ways that God desires to interact with us and show up on planet earth. Our present plight is tied into the fact that we have attempted to function in these areas without inviting Him in and asking for His solutions. We have operated as orphans who have to figure it all out on our own, when He provides Himself as the operating systems for the institutions of our nations. As we recognize Him in a healed and expanded way (which we will address in future chapters more thoroughly), and as we invite Him into the structures of society, we allow for the glory of God to be released in the earth. This is not some ethereal glory that people sing about in church. Another word for glory is reputation. The glory of God is the real God—not who we think He is based on our limited perceptions, but His correct reputation of His true heart for us and all of creation.

Jesus modeled for us a correction of the distorted view of God that dominated even the most holy of the time period He lived in. No one was further from God than the experts on God of Jesus' day. The Pharisees, the scribes, and even the priests were distorting and thus representing a grotesque perspective of God, and that false representation poisoned society. Today there is a similarity in that the proponents of God are sometimes the greatest distorters of who He is. He is waiting to be discovered as a God who is worthy of relationship—our love, trust, and adoration. He is not Santa Claus, just sitting around looking for ways to spoil us rotten, but neither is He the petulant, religious,

---

17 For more in-depth teaching on the seven main areas of culture, you can read my two books *The Seven Mountain Prophecy* and *The Seven Mountain Mantle*.

demanding, perfectionist God many supposed experts on God have implied Him to be. It is time for a fresh look at God, because what we think about Him is the most important thing about us.

We will go chapter by chapter and take an expanded look at the nuances of who God is and how He has designed our structures to function. For now, the point we want to make is this: when God said to Noah, "Whenever the rainbow appears, I will remember My covenant," what He is saying is profound and far-reaching. Basically God is saying, "I know you are continually prone toward evil, but when I look at the rainbow I will remind Myself of who I AM and of how all sufficient I AM. I will remind Myself that though humanity tends to evil, you will eventually begin to get who I am as I continually showcase who I AM."

God will have an army of sons and daughters who will stop seeing Him in such limited ways and will re-image Him in society in His full spectrum. He won't need to think only of starting over, because once Jesus came to earth, He began to expand the limited view human beings had of who God is, and everything began to change. Jesus showed us His correct reputation as a God who cares, a God who weeps, a God who laughs, a God who is engaged with society. And a God who loves, seven colors deep.

CHAPTER TWO

THE SEVEN COLORS OF LOVE

Prophet. Teacher. Saint. Mary's son. A good man who lived a long time ago who has something to do with the Bible. Son of God. The scrawny guy hanging on a cross. JESUS.

Jesus ... as if the subject of God isn't controversial enough! It appears that, as a society, we have learned how to navigate the politically correct waters of the God topic. God is love, right? Love is fairly harmless to believe in and talk about. But what about Jesus? Now there's a name that surfaces a swirl of opinions for sure. I love the way Bono, the world famous musical artist from the band U2, describes Him:

"The secular response to the Christ story always goes like this: he was a great prophet, obviously a very interesting guy, had a lot to say along the lines of other great prophets, be they Elijah, Muhammad, Buddha, or Confucius. But actually Christ doesn't allow you that. He doesn't let you off that hook. Christ says: No. I'm not saying I'm a teacher, don't call me teacher. I'm not saying I'm a prophet. I'm saying: "I'm the Messiah." I'm saying: "I am God incarnate." ... what you're left with is: either Christ was who He said He was, the Messiah, or a complete nutcase. I mean, we're talking nutcase on the level

of Charles Manson. The idea that the entire course of civilization for over half of the globe could have its fate changed and
turned upside-down by a nutcase, for me, that's farfetched!
...If only we could be a bit more like Him, the world would
be transformed. When I look at the Cross of Christ, what I see
up there is all my sin—and everybody else's. So I ask myself a
question a lot of people have asked: Who is this man? And was
He who He said He was, or was He just a religious nut? And
there it is, and that's the question. And no one can talk you
into it or out of it." [1]

*Jesus asked His close friends, "Who do you say that I am?"[2] It seems
even Jesus Himself was curious about what people thought of Him and who
they thought He was. Whether you believe He was the Son of God or not, He
clearly lived on earth and created quite a controversy with things He said and
did, died on a cross just outside of Jerusalem, and there was a hubbub about
why His body wasn't in the tomb after three days. This is historically rock
solid. So the question for you now is not whether He existed, but rather what
are you going to do about it?*

*Whether you have spoken His name with deep gratitude or let it roll off
your tongue when you stubbed your toe, you have a relationship with Him.
Not to choose is to choose. One way or another, He matters to your world. You
may have a strong opinion of Him, not based on personal knowledge but on
how others have portrayed Him. It is a huge understatement to say that much
evil has been done to countless people in His name. It is also an understatement to say that He had nothing to do with it Himself.*

*In order to expand our perspective of God, the subject of Jesus simply can-
not be ignored. Historical accounts in the Bible tell us that Jesus Himself said
the reason He came was to restore relationship between us and God by dealing
with our sin and to show us what our Father is like. He said that when we see*

---

1   from *Bono: In Conversation with Michka Assayas*, 2005
2   Matthew 16:15

Him, it is the same as seeing the Father,[3] which, by the way, is what got Jesus into so much trouble with the religious people of His time. Jesus also made it clear that of all that He did in His short life, He only did what He saw the Father wanted Him to do.[4] He literally lived and died to give us an expanded view of God.[5]

WRESTLING WITH LOVE

First, I (Elizabeth) would like to share with you some of my personal answers to many of those difficult and painful questions we presented in the introduction. Like Johnny, I was raised in a Christian home. I cannot remember life apart from a relationship with God. My parents were young Christians when my mother was diagnosed with cancer. They were courageous enough to believe that God's heart was not okay with this, so they fought in every way they could, including believing Him for her healing. After a long battle, many treatments, surgeries, and faith that could move mountains, my mom died when I was 12. I remember making a conscious choice; I will not allow myself to grow bitter with You, God, if You will do so much in my life through this that I am actually thankful I went through it. That was saying a lot. Who would ever be thankful their mother died?

I went on to tell Him that I needed Him to make my love for Him more than the pain I felt over her being gone. That was asking for a lot. I know this sounds strange, but looking back, I realize that I wasn't willing to let go of the pain because it felt like the ache I had for her was all I had left of her. I instinctively knew that if I were to have a thriving relationship with God, I needed to at least have my passion for Him be stronger than that ache. I can honestly say that He did just what I asked. I can't explain it other than He put me on a journey where I have found Him to be so good, that I am actually thankful my mother went through all she did and had her life cut short so that I could learn and feast on the reality of who God really is. I really don't think anyone

---

3   John 14:9
4   John 5:19, 17:25
5   Colossians 2:9

can get there apart from pain. We all have it, so use it wisely. What will you spend your pain on?

Because I chose not to let go of that grief for many years, I was able to stuff the pain pretty deep. I was mostly happy, except for moments when it looked like I wouldn't be able to precisely order my world around me or control things enough to keep myself and the people I loved from experiencing pain. I was also exhausted because it takes a lot of work to hold pain in and protect it like a treasure. And it's not pretty to watch; just ask my kids! When, like a good Father, God didn't rescue me and the ones I love from more pain and crisis, the things I went through as an adult became like pounding on an unhealed, hidden wound. Between raising our four daughters, helping Johnny pastor our church, and traveling with Him internationally, I used a good bit of my time and energy wrestling with God over whether or not He was good and should be trusted—whether or not He really loved me. Every circumstance was a measurement of His care for me. Watching the news on TV was overwhelming, as every crisis presented further evidence that God is a huge disappointment. I believed in Him, which left me to conclude that He is extremely distant and definitely needing me and others to carry all the weight of the world's problems. I'm tired just thinking about it! I would love to share with you what understanding came from all the questioning I went through . . .

THE BATTLE FOR INTIMACY

Ever since I was little, I heard the story of Creation. How God made the earth, Adam and Eve, and all the animals. You may think I'm foolish to believe such a tale, but for me, it takes more faith to believe in the other options I've heard! Clearly living things change and evolve to some extent, but only in an adapting kind of way that I believe God Himself put into His creation. We can put a cup of water on a table between the two of us and discuss, debate, and argue all day long about whether or not it is hot or cold. Or we can just stick our finger in it and know.

*Faith is fundamental to a relationship with God through Jesus, but experience takes you somewhere that nothing can reverse. If you haven't "put your finger in it" yet, I dare you to. I dare you to throw caution and fear of disappointment to the wind and talk to God out loud. Tell Him what you really think—about Him, about Jesus. Whatever that is, just be honest, even if your questions are full of anger and resentment. If He is God, I believe His chest is plenty big enough for you to beat on. But don't stop there. Tell Him you want to know the truth. To experience the truth. Admit to Him that if He is real, you realize He would be kind enough and capable of showing you (in just the way that **you** can get it) that He is real, that He sent Jesus as His Son for you, and that He wants a relationship with you. I dare you (said with a smile on my face). He alone knows what it will take for you to see Him as He really is, and it's not usually in a way we think or prefer. How tragic would it be if He is real and you never knew it? For now, forget even the reality of hell. What about missing a whole life with Him now? Personally, I can't think of anything in all of life more tragic than love that is given but not received. Seriously, how tragic to think that all the love your heart has craved was right in front of you, but you never experienced it.*

Back to the subject of Creation…the biblical account explains how God put Adam and Eve in a garden and gave them specific instructions not to eat the fruit of one particular tree, the tree of the knowledge of good and evil. Evidently this was no ordinary tree, but one that had supernatural fruit that, when eaten, had the potential to produce results that could affect humanity forward to all generations. The tree of the knowledge of good and evil basically gave the one who ate of it the ability to reason and perceive if something or someone is good or evil. Never before had Adam and Eve thought of anything, and more specifically of God, as being good or evil. Before the fateful day when they broke God's one rule for them, Adam and Eve didn't have the ability to doubt God or His love because they were unable to reason about whether something was good or evil. Doubting Him and His perception of them had never been an option. At the moment they ate that forbidden fruit, you and I were no better off than they were—the ones who knew God in a way that is so profound, we can easily miss it. God literally went on long walks with Adam and Eve every day and they talked and enjoyed each other. What does this tell us about our Creator?

Many of us have accepted the reality that God exists and even that He knows everything about us. But do we realize that all God has ever really wanted, from the beginning of humanity's existence, is for us to know Him? He wants to be known. The God of the universe wants to be known. If the Creator of all life wants to be known so badly, just why doesn't He sign His artwork? Maybe He should have put His signature on every sunset or His stamp of quality on every baby's bottom. Maybe He could have at least put some kind of obvious declaration of authenticity on the Bible! Maybe He is up to something far more grand than to be so obvious.

And another thing: if God is so smart (and He is), then why did He put the tree that He knew they would eat in the garden to begin with? In case you are tempted to wonder what something so long ago has to do with you right now, believe me it does. What played out there has played out in hearts through every generation and race, every economic status, in both males and females. We want a God that loves us but doesn't control us. We want a God that we can move with our tears and cries of help, but we don't want Him to need anything from us. We want Him to hold us, but we don't want to be held.

*Does that make us evil? No, it just makes us prone to distance ourselves from Him. Does that make us normal? Yes, as normal as He knew we would be when He put the tree in the garden to begin with. If He had not given us the option of **choice**, then there was no potential for **trust**. Trust is only real to the degree it is given the opportunity to choose.*

*Why did God care about trust between Himself and humanity's first representation on earth? Because without trust, there is no true **intimacy**. An intimate relationship cannot exist apart from trust. In intimacy there is a mutual knowing of each other and no walls hiding the truth of who you really are. God created us for intimacy with Him, and that intimacy is something He is too kind and loving to force on us by choosing for us. He wants intimacy* *with us so badly that when He gets it, He wants it to be real, which can only happen in the context of the freedom of choice. He wants you to know Him, like He knows you. He wants a real and intimate relationship with you. For all of eternity. What do you think about that?*

Stand in front of that tree with me for a minute. Just like Adam and Eve did, taste that sweet supernatural fruit—the evidence of an invitation to intimacy with your Creator is in your hand, just like it was in theirs. Feel the reality of what happened when doubt became a possibility, hitting you full on. The "what ifs" that we are all familiar with come rushing in—our distorted perception of His intentions towards us. What if all the hard things I have been through mean He doesn't care or doesn't really love me? What if the fact that He didn't step in and keep _____ from happening means that He isn't good and shouldn't be trusted? What if the fact that I can't hear Him speak to me means He is silent, and maybe that silence is proof that I am a bother to Him? What if I have been so bad that He has rejected me? What if He isn't real at all?

The repercussions of just one bite were huge, to the point that evidently it literally changed the DNA that we inherited from Adam and Eve ever since. We can't be too mad with them, though. You and I would have made the same choice! Knowing the God I've come to know, I have to believe that He wasn't surprised by their choice. Disappointed yes, but not surprised or sorry. He sees the beginning from the end and knew that His plan B would be even better than plan A. His ability to redeem, to make things better for us, is so thorough that He makes it even better than it would have been. The key in all of life, whether we are talking about our soul or a situation, is to invite Him in to do what He is good at: redeeming. He values true intimacy with us so much that we must invite Him. He simply will not insist. If you don't see evidence of HIm as a good Father in your life, then it is for certain that you have not invited Him in as Redeemer. It may take time, but without fail, He loves to show us His true heart. He loves for us to know Him just like He knows us, with nothing between us but truth.

From our limited perspective as humans, Jesus was God's Plan B, but not really. With the exception of how long God seems to be taking to unfold

His plan, I am continually in awe of what He is doing. When you really get what Jesus' life and the cross were all about, the love story that we are a part of is the best that has ever been thought of with the happiest ending (or beginning, depending on how you look at it) that will ever be told. As with all good stories, there must be something other-worldly about it, and there must be an enemy to be defeated.

THE ENEMY OF GOD

I remember a friend in college who didn't believe in God until one night when he saw demons in plain sight for the first time.[6] Bam. Just like that, he was front and center on the stage of the biggest production of all — drawn into the battle for intimacy with his Creator. Nothing I could have said would have convinced him like he was when he met pure evil. As a guy who had an appreciation for philosophy, it meant one thing to him: pure good existed too. God was real after all. Even if we prefer not to acknowledge it because of fear, we are spirits living in a natural physical body, but we exist in the context of a supernatural realm. The natural is obviously real, as are the laws of nature. But supernatural supersedes the natural. God created both, so whenever He wants to, He can supersede the natural with the even more real supernatural realm that we are a part of. You may be more comfortable with what you can see and touch, but be certain of this: what we cannot readily see and touch is more real. Our spirits came into the natural realm from the spirit realm and will one day return back to that realm.

If God is real (and He is), then He, by His very name that defines Him, is all-powerful. There is none above Him, including His enemy. There is one enemy of God. (I don't like to miss rabbit trails when at all possible, as I am sure you can tell, but I will leave this one and move forward as if you easily agree with me.) God's enemy is called Satan, or sometimes Lucifer. Not much

---

6   Not only is Satan real, but demons are too. Many, like my friend, have seen them just as real as a person. The Bible explains that in heaven, before creation, Satan rebelled against God and a third of the angels fell away from God as well, those that we now call demons (Revelation 12:4).

is known about him before creation, but there are several things we do know. He is as real as God is (just ask my college friend). There is no comparison between him and God. God is everything that His enemy is not.

Something happened that caused Satan to hate God with a rage we cannot fathom but have definitely seen and felt the collateral damage from. When an enemy loathes its target so completely but cannot touch him, he is left with one option: go after the object of God's love and affection. And that would be you and me. For those of you who are parents, you know that there is nothing that can hurt you more than to see your children hurting. For a perfect Father whose motivation is the truest, purest expression of selfless love, nothing could wound more deeply than for His child to believe anything less than the truth about His heart for them. When intimacy is the desire, the lack of it feels catastrophic. We all know what that feels like because we are made in the image of a Father who knew that ache for intimacy long before we did.

In the garden, if you remember the story, it was Satan who tempted Eve to eat the fruit from the one tree of the knowledge of good and evil that God said not to eat. Satan attempted to make sure, for Adam and Eve and the rest of humanity after them, that we would forever stay stuck in a cycle of doubt about our Father's true heart towards us—doubt about whether or not He is good or evil. He set into motion a chain reaction of lies about this God of love that we still wrestle with today. Jesus called this enemy the Father of Lies. When the poison is a lie, the antidote is the truth. When the lies cause a false, narrow perspective of who God is, only the correct reputation or glory of God can bring truth and restore intimacy and the true knowledge of Him.

Jesus is that truth. Jesus Himself lived in such a way that we could see the truth about what God is really like. If you have never read the Bible, or perhaps tried to but didn't get too far, consider reading about the life of Jesus. The book of John is a great place to start. If you have known God for many years, but, like I was, aren't sure of how good He actually is, then read the Bible with new "glasses" on from a fresh perspective. Read with the assumption that you have been told a lie that has been sown into your DNA by the enemy of God back in the garden. Read with the opposite assumption of how life's circumstances have made you feel. I'm not saying to ignore your experi-

ences. I'm saying to bring them under a different light. Read what Jesus said and did, looking for proof that you have perhaps believed some lies *about your God because of what you have seen and experienced in your* life.

I believe Adam and Eve's brains literally changed, giving them the capability to reason and doubt and we, of course, inherited that "skill" as well. We are so afraid of absolute truth, but that is the remedy for absolute lies. Every day, since before we drew our first breath, we are bombarded with circumstances and painful realities that, when filtered through our forbidden-fruit-filled brains and limited perspectives of God, cause us to doubt His goodness and love. If we are still able to perceive Him at all, He appears in one color, and somehow it's rarely the color of love.

The enemy of God has no true power over God, so why doesn't God just override His destruction and lies? Why wouldn't everyone who is greater than their enemies not completely annihilate them? God has reasons that are not clear to us, but it must have something to do with His ultimate plans for us. He is obviously using Satan as a pawn to accomplish what is going to prove out to be for our long-term good.

To sum it all up, because Adam and Eve ate of that tree, we are wired to perceive God wrongly based on the difficult things we go through. God knew that would happen and didn't prevent it because He knew that would present the possibility for trust, and therefore the potential for His ultimate goal: intimacy with His sons and daughters. Why do bad things happen (either because of our own choices or because of Satan's evil) and God seems to do little if anything about it? Why would good parents allow their child to suffer? The answer to both is obvious if you are certain He, or the parent, is indeed good. He is aware of something we, or the child, is not aware of—a bigger picture with a greater reward than immediate relief, a context that is much broader than what seems apparent. You've heard God wants to prepare us to get to eternity, but what about preparing us for what we will **do** *in eternity? A child is allowed by a good parent to go through suffering and pain when the parent is aware that something of greater worth is to follow. It's all about trust and what we cannot see. It's all about intimacy that follows trust.*

Consider this: What if you chose to believe that God is r̶ is good, no matter what? For a change, begin to look at ever through and what you watch others go through in a new way whatever God does or doesn't do, that you wish He would or wouldn't do, is wholly motivated by His love. My favorite definition of hope is from a friend of ours, Bob Hartley. He says hope is the anticipation of good from God in all areas of life. What would life be like if we never lost hope? What would it be like if we perceived everything through the eyes of hope—through the belief that God is good and only good.

Suppose I'm right about this, or even just some of it. If there is a battle for intimacy, based on God's deep longing to have relationship with us and to be known like He knows us; and if there is an enemy who wants to hurt the heart of this perfect Father by convincing us that He is not so good; then the ultimate defeat to this foe who has made our lives and most of this world miserable is that we would find intimacy with our God and know the goodness of our Father. Know the real Him and know Him so well that we show others the real Him. Real love. Love displayed in every color, in every aspect of life and culture. If the threat is the squelching of His true identity, then let's be more determined than any other generation to know the real Him, the fullness of who He is, and shout it from every high and low place, painting with broad strokes with every color that He is.

INVITE HIM IN

Jesus spent a lot of time traveling from town to town healing people who were sick and teaching all who wanted to hear about what God and His kingdom are like. One particular day He taught them how to talk to God. Most people then, like now, were all too familiar with and turned off by the religious ones who made prayer seem so insincere and contrived. Jesus knew that people then, like us, were interested in authenticity. Most of you have probably heard and maybe even memorized the Lord's Prayer. Once again, Jesus was intent on helping all of us, the sons and daughters of God, relate to the one He *knew as Father so we could also know the real God. Before Jesus gave them an idea of how to pray, He explained how not to pray. I love the way* The Message [7] *translation says it:*

"The world is full of so-called prayer warriors who are prayer-ignorant. They're full of formulas and programs and advice, peddling techniques for getting what you want from God. Don't fall for that nonsense. This is your Father you are dealing with, and He knows better than you what you need. With a God like this loving you, you can pray very simply. Like this: [8]

"Our Father in heaven,
  Hallowed be Your name.
  Your kingdom come.
  Your will be done, on earth as it is in heaven.
  Give us this day our daily bread.
  And forgive us our debts, as we forgive our debtors.
  And do not lead us into temptation, but deliver us from
      the evil one.
  For Yours is the kingdom and the power
      and the glory forever. Amen."[9]

I've read this prayer and prayed it many times, but it wasn't until recently that I noticed the seven areas that it touches on as it relates to an expanded perspective of God. Jesus was and is so profound in His simplicity. Just like His Father. It appears at first glance that He is saying one thing, but then when you look at it from another angle, there is yet another level of truth to be seen. In fact, as many angles as you can look at Him and what He said and did, there are equally as many ways He can make us stand amazed at Him and the truth that He spoke and continues to speak, if we have ears to hear.

---

7 *The Message* by Eugene Peterson, NavPress, 2002.
8 Matthew 6:7-9 The Message Translation
9 Matthew 6:9-13

In each of the next seven chapters, we will discover an expanded perspective of the heart of a God who loves us in every way that He can offer Himself. We will also process through the lies we believe about that aspect of God and the ways those lies play out in the culture of our personal lives and nations. And, of course, we will focus on the truth of who God is as each color of the rainbow that He Himself chose to represent as the real Him. *A segment at the end of each chapter will challenge you line by line from the Lord's Prayer (above) to pray or talk to the God of all of life and invite Him into the places you need Him the most. Think of this part of each chapter as a way to not just read a book, but to actually respond and actively expand your perspective of who God is to you.*

The truth is, He can be known. You can know Him. You can know His love. You can watch Him color outside the religious lines with all the colors of the rainbow. You probably already know Him better than you think you do—you just have to learn to see Him as the seven colors of love.

CHAPTER THREE

PAPA: The Color of Strength
THE SOLUTION FOR OUR FAMILIES

The words father, dad, daddy, abba, and papa stir up as many different feelings as the number of people who use them. Every person has one, and every person has had their own unique experience with their father—or lack of one. As we established earlier, what you think of God is the most important thing about you. It's no less true in the family sense as well. What a child thinks about his or her father is more important and can have more impact than any other dynamic in the family. In an ideal world (which, by the way, doesn't exist), the presence of a good father was meant to provide strength to the children and a stable home to launch them into life. Family was meant to be a tangible illustration of the very real strength that God is for His children.

As mentioned previously, colors are generally known to evoke a variety of feelings or moods. We tend to associate certain colors with memorable objects or events. For example, most of us think of the color orange as a happy color and associate it with a citrus fruit, the orange. For those who live in a region that experiences seasonal changes, it may also provoke memories of fall, when leaves display gorgeous shades of golden and fiery oranges. In each chapter, as we position ourselves to see God with an expanded view, we'll look at Him as Rainbow God, the God of all of life in His many colors.

We'll also look at Him through the seven main areas of culture and how He offers Himself to us—the "face" of His nature that becomes the very solution to the problems that are prevalent in that area of life. For example, in this chapter we will look at the area of culture we will refer to as Family and how God has given us the opportunity to know Him as our Father and our strength for all the problems we face related to the breakdown of families in society. For those of you who may be concerned about our biblical basis for making these connections, don't worry; we aren't trying to establish doctrine but are simply using these as a context in which to speak of the amazing attributes of God.

When we speak of God as Father, it's not quite the same as what we normally think of in the traditional sense—the man who is our father by birth. The Bible described creation like this:

"God created man in His own image; in the image of God He created him; male and female He created them."[1]

This was right before God formed Adam, the first human—just like us, minus a belly button. Notice how it says that God made Adam in His image, male and female. And of course, soon after, God took out a part of Adam (his rib) and used it to create Eve. Basically, God created the full image of Himself as male and female in Adam, and then separated His full image into a male and a female so that together they would bear His full image on earth. When we talk about God as our Father we are actually speaking of Him as a complete set of parents wrapped up into one—Papa God. You can call Him Father or your version of a dad, but we have grown accustomed to calling Him Papa as a term of endearment and an attempt to steer our hearts away from the more typically religious term of Father. He loves it no matter what His sons and daughters call Him, as long as we acknowledge that we are His. In the same way that our identity, or lack of, is given to us by our father and mother, so too is our spiritual identity given to us by our Heavenly Father,

---

1   Genesis 1:27

who is summed up as both male and female. Again, ideally God's heart for us is that we would have a mother and a father in our life who together make up a complete perspective of what He is like. That's one of the reasons why Johnny and I are so glad we could write this particular book together. There's something powerful when men and women work together in unity to accomplish something, as it seems to give a more complete interpretation or outlook on a matter.

LOVE DISPLAYED AS STRENGTH

Orange is the color of **strength** and we use it to refer to the sector or structure of society called **family**. Family is the foundational fabric of every nation. Without family, there is no fabric of society. To the degree families are fractured and frayed, society is fractured and frayed. *We chose the color orange to represent family because it's made from a mixture of red and yellow. Red can speak of our family bloodline and yellow of our individual unique glory—what makes us who we are (which we will talk more about in the chapter on yellow, the color of glory). Orange represents that part of our Papa's heart that affirms that yes, we belong to Him. We are His bloodline. Whatever else you may or may not discover about who you are, always know that you are His and you belong in the family of God. It also represents the fact that He not only made each of us to be unique, He also enjoys what makes you who you are. We each have our own glory or distinct beauty that delights and makes proud the heart of this Father.*

God is love, and not only does He care for our families, the idea of families originated in Him. So what does He, as love, look like in families? **In a family, love looks like strength.** *Strength that stands against the storms of life when everything else falls apart. The one thing you can always come back to.*

A man or woman founded on a healthy family is a strong individual. Of course, strength can still be found in a spiritual family and in friends when there is a breakdown of a person's natural family. But God's first preference is that our natural families provide us with a stable, loving, and secure environment to grow in. He alone is the perfect Papa, and He loves each and every one of us exceedingly above and beyond what we could imagine. This love, and wherever it finds its expression, is our strength. If you have experienced true love of any sort through any source, it came from Him and Him alone. God doesn't just love us. He IS love. And when you find this love, you find your strength. You and I were created to know Him—to know love. To be loved. To never know a breath in this realm apart from knowing, in every cell of our being and in every corner of our heart, that we are loved with a perfect love, unconditionally.

When the strength of family is weakened, the purposes God created family for are lost: protection, procreation, provision, instruction, and identity. When these become eroded, our families are weak, we are weak, and our nations are weak. When we experience each of these purposes for family in a healthy way, we have the opportunity to experience the love of God. When we don't, doors are left open for lies to come creeping in about our Papa's heart toward us. When we aren't protected by our family, we believe we aren't safe. When we aren't properly provided for and protected, we believe we aren't worth caring for and being protected. When we are left to figure life out for ourselves, we believe we must be a burden and are too complicated to deal with. And when our true identity is not spoken into our hearts, we believe we have none. All of these lies draw us to one conclusion: we have been abandoned and rejected by God. But as we will discover, love is stronger than lies.

THE LIE:
WE HAVE BEEN ABANDONED
AND REJECTED BY GOD

Satan advances his initial work of undermining families through the use of one basic instrument and strategy, one basic lie. That strategy or lie is **rejection.** He uses the fact that our very first encounters with family and life come while we are still in the womb, from before the time we are born. From the moment we are conceived, because we carry within us the spirit of the One he loathes, Satan begins whispering the lie of all lies—you are not wanted. Remember, how can an enemy ultimately cause the most pain to a good father's heart? Make His children doubt how much He really loves and cares for them.

For instance, I (Johnny) believe every time an infant in a womb hears an argument, a demonically sourced lie is sown into that child's heart—"They are arguing about you. You must not be wanted." Research has proven that babies in the womb respond to sounds and stress that the mother is exposed to. Knowing that, I believe Satan's demons work overtime to convince infants and young children that they are rejected. He knows that if he can get us to believe our natural parents have rejected us, then we are more prone to believe our Father in heaven has rejected us too. If children experience real rejection, then the enemy's job is even easier because he is only speaking what is true. However, demons will often use their influence to convince a very loved and accepted child that they are rejected, and if that person's heart agrees with that lie, they can do as much damage in that person as in a person who really was rejected. Even the most loving parents may for a moment lose their cool and make a child feel as if he or she isn't wanted or loved. You can be sure a demon will be there offering lies to the heart that believes.

Ultimately, rejection, whether real or perceived, is the root problem for the vast majority of all family issues. Those who feel rejected will reject others, or even aspects of themselves. I believe that many reject their own sexuality as an extension of either experiencing rejection or believing the lie that they have been rejected. Often the enemy uses sexual abuse as part of his plan to wound us and cause us to reject our original sexuality.

I would never want to say anything that makes gays feel more rejection than they already do from much of society. But I do believe that, by and large, there is a root wound of rejection that was caused very early in life in the hearts of gays. Why do they want acceptance so much so that they have organized and brought more change to our culture in one generation than most other action groups? Because they have suffered such profound rejection. Is it really helpful for Christians to add to that wound? Why do we feel such strong conviction to make it clear to gays, lesbians, bisexuals, and transvestites that their lifestyle is a sin, but we are not so upfront with our convictions about adultery and addiction to porn? Are we really so concerned for "the standard" that we can't show love and acceptance of them as people?

I know this can be a complicated, multifaceted issue with some aggressive gay activists and equally aggressive and legalistic religious zealots muddying the water, making it difficult for a balanced perspective. Let me just reiterate, though, that the core issue is rejection. I suggest that, based on that knowledge, we honestly seek Papa God's heart for solutions and strategies for how to heal that rejection, rather than simply focusing on a standard. Do I believe that homosexuality is a sin? The Bible clearly states it is, but also clearly states that our position is not to be one of judgment, but of love. We Christians often forget that the reason God even cares about sin is because He cares about us. So when we focus on upholding a standard of sin, rather than a standard of love, we are not correctly reflecting His heart to the gay community. When any of us are living a lifestyle that He sees as sin, He will convict us personally. That leaves us free to love each other and trust that, as our Father, He will lead us to feel conviction that leads to freedom if we are locked into something that has affected our intimacy with Him. If His kindness leads us to repent, then how much more so should we represent Him to each other through kindness. Some may argue that if we are truly kind, then we will make sure someone knows that what they are doing is sin. I believe the religious of our generation have already made that loud and clear and now it's time to learn to love and be kind.

HOW DOES THIS LIE ABOUT GOD
PLAY OUT IN CULTURE?

If the lie about God is that He has abandoned and rejected us, then how does that play out in culture? How does the present reality of most families perpetuate this particular lie about God? Rejection, like all good lies, just needs one small entrance and can settle in as a never ending cycle, generation after generation. If we don't recognize the lie for what it is, then our hurt causes us to hurt others. When we feel rejected, the reason it hurts like no other pain on earth is because of what it subconsciously and ultimately communicates to our heart, that God doesn't love us. No human can live a quality life under the core belief that the One who created them doesn't truly care for them. The pain of rejection plays out in further rejection of others. To some degree, we all suffer from a level of rejection and therefore tend to judge and reject each other. Families become a haven for this lie and we grow up not only feeling rejected, but learning to reject others as some sort of dysfunctional survival mechanism. Kids feel rejected by parents, then grow up to cause their kids to feel rejected. Families and individuals transfer that culture of rejection to the larger stage of people groups, religions, races, and economic statuses. Rejection in the home and personal level breeds rejection in every layer of society.

In the landscape of life today, no institution stands in greater need of heaven's intervention than the family. We need God as Papa, the family man, not only to fill the void that has been left in so many hearts but also to give us His strategies for restoring back to our cultures what family was originally meant to be. Somehow, even in our religious institutions, and even among our religious leaders, we're experiencing tremendous challenges to the family unit. Divorce, sexual abuse, verbal and emotional abuse, violence, and abortion are rampant everywhere. These realities are creating more and more fractured individuals, which are themselves then producing more fractured and dysfunctional people. "Normal" doesn't seem to exist anymore, and aberrant symptoms of this brokenness appear to be only increasing. It looks as if no one wants to embrace a standard, and then even those who do embrace standards fail miserably, heaping upon themselves the tag of "hypocrite." Every statistical analysis of family realities is more and more dire. It seems we are hopelessly in way over our heads in knowing what to do or how to correct this massive societal problem.

So who's to blame for the breakdown of families in society? I don't believe there's just one answer. Some want to blame gays for what they see as an aggressive agenda—adopting children, bringing LGBT curriculum into education, redefining marriage, finding a role in every TV show, and more. Yet statistically the gay community may only account for as little as 2 percent of the population. So how does their "agenda" cause Christians to divorce at more than a 50 percent ratio? If all gays moved to their own island, would our family crisis go with them? I think the evidence is clear that it would not. Maybe we should stop scapegoating gays.

Others believe the problem is that we just don't understand covenant anymore. We don't know how to commit like people did in past generations. The problem seems to be that we're divorcing too much, and divorce is devastating for kids. This is at least partially true and for sure a piece of the overall puzzle of brokenness that we're experiencing.

But I (Johnny) contend that bettering the divorce rates would still reveal that a lack of commitment is not our only indicator for family health. Though God hates divorce, I surely identify as a father with a God who hates a long list of conditions that *cause* divorce. As horrible as divorce is, there are things that are worse. Maybe because I have four daughters, I feel entitled to consider how God would feel toward His daughters who are in abusive marriages. If I were God and my son-in-law was beating my daughter, I would hate that abuse even more than I hate divorce. I would want that man out of the house. He would be fortunate I didn't shoot him—even though I hate divorce. Neither would I want my daughters married to a drug addict or a porn addict. I hate divorce, but I can't imagine watching my grand-kids grow up in that kind of setting. Nor would I want one of my daughters married to a man who verbally abuses her, nor to one who treats her as if she were his slave. (I'm confident that other parents can identify with this.) Does our Papa God really hate divorce more than He would hate 40 or 50 years of this kind of misery and jeopardy for His daughters? Why is it that men always seem to be the hardliners against divorce? Is that still a manifestation of the performance thing above the heart thing? The Bible itself adds that a man who doesn't provide for his household is worse than an infidel, one who is consid-ered unfaithful to God. It seems as if God really hates that too. What happens when God hates the entire array of realities? Is there possibly a mercy option? *The answer is yes. God spoke it loud and clear through the life of Jesus. Through the many accounts we have of His interactions with broken imperfect people, we see that Jesus, and therefore our Father, always offers mercy to us.*

If our only solution for making families stronger is to oppose di-vorce or reduce the divorce rate, then maybe we should all become Muslims or Hindus. They have a much lower divorce rate. Wherever a woman is considered the property of a man, you will see lower divorce statistics, but that doesn't necessarily mean there are good marriages. However, I also contend that one of the immediate effects of women being given proper value and legally validated and sup-ported in society is an increase in the divorce rate. I think it will hap-pen every time a society makes advancements in freedom. If we could keep women as slaves, the divorce rate could perhaps go down to zero, right? Clearly I don't intend for anyone to take that sentence out of context. But it does demonstrate the ridiculous ways we tend to reason about these things.

I was recently traveling in another country and spoke with pas-tors there who were greatly concerned because, as their society has become more Christian, divorces have exponentially increased. Isn't it a problem that when we find Christianity becomes more prevalent in societies that oppress women, the divorce rate goes up? Do we give up on Christianity? Or is it maybe that the precepts of Christ validate and liberate women? The Bible is clear that males are not superior to females[2]. An intended message of Christianity is that we each have tremendous worth and value to God. Would it not then be natural for women who embrace this to then cease to be okay with being cheated on, beaten, abused, or otherwise demeaned? Is it supposed to be healthy for kids to grow up under those offenses as long as there is no divorce? Do we really believe in a God that would sacrifice the lives of many of His daughters just so His standard remains intact? Christians, can we please serve and represent a God who not only has a recommended standard of commitment but also has rules of healthy boundaries and integrous behavior within that covenant?

My intention is not to be a proponent of divorce but simply to say that we have to look deeper than we have when we're addressing the issue of family breakdown. We really do have to stop judging each other by surface statistics that don't answer all the underlying realities. Women clearly will bail out of a marriage quicker now that they have the freedom to take care of their own financial future, unlike past generations. Should we then disallow women from working outside the home because it's a statistical cause of divorce? I know some believe that, but again, is the idea to force women to stay with men even when they are egregiously mistreated? I think it's safe to say we want men and women to quit divorcing over frivolous squabbles or just because they are bored. There's nothing wrong with opposing a casual approach to marriage. But I don't think we want to be saying that divorce at all costs must be stopped. There are just too many other ingredients in the mix.

In order to reject, we must first judge if something or someone should be rejected. We have all done it without even thinking about it. Jesus, who knew the heart of Papa God better than any of us, spoke constantly about love, but

---

2   Galatians 3:28

never did He encourage us to size someone up based on their behavior and treat them in a way that would cause them to feel unloved, judged, or rejected. Many Christians say, "Love the sinner, hate the sin." What if we were to love the sinner (starting with ourselves) and that's it? If we considered our right to love others as children of God as greater than our right to protect and uphold our moral values, then this lie that God has rejected us may actually begin to unravel.

THERE IS ONE ENEMY IN THE WAR OVER FAMILIES

Satan is at high-level war against the foundation of society. You may not want to believe it's that simple—some evil supernatural force trying to corrode us from the inside out. But it really is that simple. Surely you have experienced it yourself all those times you move forward only to be continually knocked back down. Convince me that we aren't caught in the frontline of a spiritual war zone. Convince the millions who don't have all the many ways we do in Western cultures to ignore the full impact of his destruction. Even those who would say they don't have a relationship with God are at times quick to blame Him when things go wrong. If you are capable of believing that, then why not also acknowledge the reality of a real enemy and blame him? In each aspect of who God is, we will see that although He has only one enemy, that enemy shows himself in many ways and brings his war to many battle fronts with his fairly simple but varied lies about our God. He tries to distort God's reputation in as many ways as we'll believe and agree with him. But one truth we must embrace before we can uproot these lies is that Satan is the enemy. Not God. Not your family. Not the government or religious people. Not even yourself. When you know where the shots of gunfire are coming from, you know where they can be stopped. When you know what the ammunition being sent your way is, you know how to protect yourself from it. Though Satan finds many voices, he is the source of all lies. And your Papa is the source of all truth.

Satan does everything in his power to destroy families. He knows destroyed families will produce hurt and wounded people. And hurt and wounded people tend to hurt and wound other people, who reproduce more destroyed families. This is also a major fortress for him as he uses the heartache and stress of relational breakdowns to release sickness and disease as a byproduct of broken families. Many studies show that as much as 90 percent of all illnesses are psychosomatic and stem from a root cause that can be traced to a broken relationship, most notably the relationship with a parent. Probably the most painful broken relationship for any person is that of a father. Most autoimmune diseases are just what the description implies. In autoimmune diseases the body attacks itself, similar to the "attack" they may have experienced in their own family. The body's defenses attack the body itself instead of the enemy or foreign bodies. This and other diseases are very common for those who have grown up in a household environment where they didn't feel loved or wanted or where Satan got them to agree with that lie. Satan is a mean and vicious entity, and his job description is stealing, killing, and destroying[3] the sons and daughters of God—of which you are one, whether you realize it or feel like it. It's his way for getting back at Papa God for not permitting his treachery in heaven. In his schemes to advance pain, torment, and death, he targets every one of the sectors of society with a master plan for what would best bring destruction in that specific sector.

This war over families can appear to be over so many things that it is not. It is not over your life or your future, although it can feel quite personal at times. It is not over the politically correct definition of family. The war over families is over the correct reputation of God, your expanded and healed perspective of who He is, and what His heart as Papa is for you.

WHO IS GOD—AS PAPA?

God not only has the answers and solutions for all societal ills, but He in fact provides Himself as the solution. Over the years it has

---

3   John 10:10

grown quite cliché or trite for Christians to say "Jesus is the answer." The implication has been that no matter what you are going through, all will be okay if you will just "get saved." Reality is that this simply has not proven true. As Christians, we are usually only referring to "getting saved" as it relates to repenting of sins and accepting Jesus Christ as Lord and Savior, when it's so much more. It does satisfy the question, "Where will you spend eternity?" but it has not satisfied the question, "How do I get through life now?" Our lack of seeing a God who can fully function in society has led us to market a relationship with God that is only about acting right so you can live in heaven one day. (And as Christians ourselves, allow us to say we're sorry!) As you begin to see Him as the Rainbow God, you will become aware that not only did He create you to have a relationship with Him for eternity, He really does care about your quality of life here on earth. The full-spectrum God has an aspect of Himself that is prepared to fix every problem in society. He is Papa God, the perfect Father who is able to heal our rejection and show us how to break its devastating cycle in our culture.

THE TRUTH:
GOD HAS NOT ABANDONED OR REJECTED US

God as Papa is the only One who can heal the core wound of rejection because that wound was ultimately caused by the core belief that God has rejected and abandoned us. No matter how or through whom the enemy was able to make us feel rejection, our hearts all eventually, at least on a subconscious level, are made to feel like the One in charge should have made sure we grew up being loved and fully accepted. Even those of us who embrace a religion that tells us God is love and that He loves us struggle with the message that is opposite, based on the way we filter our circumstances and life experiences. (Back to our great-great-great grandparents Adam and Eve's desire for apple pie!)

Every other cure for rejection, other than a healthy relationship with Papa God, seems short-lived and a virtual band-aid compared to the depth of the hurt. Those who feel rejected tend to demand unusual levels of acceptance in an attempt to satisfy the wound of rejection. As stated before, their attempts usually result in more rejection, which then causes the wound to grow more painful and deeper. It enters the stage where the one feeling rejection now initiates rejection everywhere he or she goes in order to feel some sense of control over the pain and rejection cycle.

But Papa offers Himself to be our personal healer as well as our societal healer. As we take our frustration, pain, anger, and bitterness to Him, He embraces us still, and if we will let Him, He will hug the poison of the lie of rejection right out of us. No matter what level of adverse childhood you have experienced, and no matter what level of brokenness and dysfunction you carry, He offers Himself to you as Papa, the color of strength. All that's required is to let Him in. Remember, this is the key for all life—to invite God in. Let Him in. This does not mean you even have to ask Him in as Savior. You may not be ready for that yet. He values you whether you ever invite Him in as Savior or not. Many think and teach that we have no worth or value apart from God. But that just isn't true any more than a child's value to their parent only comes when they know who that parent is and what they are like. A good parent loves their child simply because the child is theirs, even before that child ever became aware of being theirs. We don't get our value when we begin a relationship with God through Jesus, but the fact that God sent Jesus to restore our relationship to Himself is proof of the value that we already have in our Papa's eyes.

God loves you unconditionally as your original Papa, more than any natural parent ever could. Put the book down and just let that soak in for a minute. He is your original Papa, and He loves you unconditionally, more than any natural parent ever could.

God thought of you before the foundation of the world, and He designed purpose and meaning into your original fabric.[4] He is the only One who has ever known all the challenges and rejections you have been through. Any voice that tells you that He just sat by, unmoved by your pain, is a lie. He preemptively designed a plan for your life where even your pain and shame could become a platform for you to know the real Him and for the Light of who He is to shine through you. In Papa's eyes, no one is ever damaged goods. He sees the end from the beginning, and He has a "better than"[5] plan for your life the moment you let Him in as Papa—better than anything you can imagine.[6]

Healed people are especially great conduits of healing for others. A person healed of rejection has an unusual ability to restore rejected people into the arms of Papa. As His healing circle expands, we see families begin to look like they are supposed to—like the kind of families God wants us to experience. A family devoid of the ravages and toxins of rejection will reproduce in like fashion.

Do you want to know what true acceptance feels like? It's not wrong to want acceptance; in fact, God put that desire in us. Why did He put it in us? Again, we were created in His image and He desires acceptance too because He Himself has a core value for intimacy and relationship. True acceptance only comes through a God-inspired encounter with God's love for you. You can feel such rejection that, without even knowing that you're doing it, you try to force people around you to respect you out of fear of some kind of backlash or manipulation. And yet that kind of acceptance will always ring hollow because it only dealt with the behavior of others and not with your inner sense of rejection. You can even get the law to punish people

---

4   Psalm 139:13
5   Again, our friend Bob Hartley has a great word picture of God as "the better than God with the better than plan." He is better than all the lesser things we settle for and His plans, in the end, are always better than what we think we want.
6   Jeremiah 29:11

for rejecting you, and your wound is still not cured. The biggest reason we dislike and "bumper sticker" against mean people is that they remind us of our core rejection wound. We believe that if we can just mute all possible voices that are against us, then we will finally feel this craved acceptance. But the truth is that acceptance can only come from Papa God, and He only waits to be allowed in past the walls you built to protect your heart from more pain and rejection to show you just how much He loves you.

HOW CAN WE COOPERATE WITH GOD AS PAPA IN RESTORING STRENGTH TO FAMILIES?

This, of course, is the desire of our Papa's heart—that His sons and daughters become so convinced of His love and acceptance and healed of their rejection that we then become carriers of healing. As our relationship with Him is restored, we can experience profound fulfillment by participating with His heart to heal families. Most disease, crime, mental illness, and aberrant lifestyles are a direct result of toxic families—families who have lost their strength. Anyone called to impact the structure of family in any nation's culture is ultimately called to be an agent of healing at every level of society possible.

Those called to advance the correct reputation of our Papa's heart will fill private and government institutions such as DFACS (Department of Family and Children Services), as these are often the first line of defense for family breakdown. Don't you think our Papa would love to have this and similar type institutions filled with sons and daughters who do this, not for the money but to be an extension of His hand and heart in society itself? Many who love God might wrongly assume that God won't use us to represent His heart unless we can give Him the credit, but that's so not like the real Him. As we said before, He is not One to sign His name to things that obviously could have only come from Him because, unlike us, He doesn't need the affirmation.

He knows that if we want truth and clarity on the source of something, we will look for it and He will be found. So consider taking your expanded perspective of this heart of God to the front lines of the war against families and shout the truth of His love without necessarily even feeling the responsibility to connect it to His name. People will know instinctively, when it's all said and done, that it's Papa's love they have hoped for all along. He will make sure. I'm not saying to keep silent about God, but rather don't limit the ways you show love just because it may not be appropriate in all settings to attribute it directly to Him.

Can you sense Papa God's heart to have our court systems filled with His sons and daughters who understand this mission to silence the lies of rejection and heal the affects of them in our families? He is raising up ones who are prepared to represent Him right where important decisions that affect families are being made. Judges who understand His heart will carry unique authority and wisdom to rightly choose between offering mercy or severity. Sometimes the severe sentence is in itself mercy, as it can serve as a needed wake up call. Other times a judge needs discernment from God to recognize that there has been true repentance and therefore offer mercy. Only God can see the hearts and know these matters for sure. Those who represent Him in these settings will learn to invite Him in, and as they do, He will empower them to restore even the most broken families.

Papa will use even those who were the most rejected and wounded of His sons and daughters to develop laws and legislation that protect and reward families economically. You may be a lawyer, judge, or politician, but in the big picture, you are called to be a champion of His love and acceptance that brings strength to our hearts and ultimately to our families. Families need help from so many angles that there are unlimited ways to bring love that heals.

Other obvious ways to work alongside Papa include being a family or marriage counselor. We can offer premarital courses specifically designed to make sure the rejection wound has received the truth of His love. We can offer childcare services that are focused on bringing

His heart of acceptance into the home or daycare center. So many aren't sure of their purpose, or that they matter. But we can know our purpose and really make a difference as we embrace the truth—that our Creator, Papa God, never abandoned us and has always accepted us as His. Then we can give that truth and that kind of love away to those who don't yet know it. What better place to start than in those early years of childcare.

I (Elizabeth) am reminded of a scene in the acclaimed movie The Help. *A black woman who served as a maid and nanny to a prejudiced white family was so rejected by society at that time, just because of the color of her skin, that she was able to recognize that the white child she cared for was being raised under equally painful rejection by her too-busy mother. Each day the nanny would say goodbye to the child, she would look her deep in the eyes and say, "You is smart. You is kind. You is important." Under her watch, she made sure that child felt all the love and acceptance she deserved because she herself knew the value of it. When we face the pain of rejection personally, we then become able to recognize it in someone else and help heal their wounds.*

Anyone who feels called to be a healer of humans in any way is ultimately called to this sector of society called Family. It means you have compassion on human suffering and you want to do your part to assist with healing pain or stop it at its source whenever possible. It also means that at some point, whether you realized it was God at the time or not, you gained an appreciation and passion for that aspect of who He is. You saw the color orange and liked it enough to add it to your "wardrobe." You might have thought it was just you stumbling into a career choice, but in actuality you stumbled into Him.

If you are involved with the medical profession, it should be because it is your heart's passion to truly help people. If you are only a doctor for the excellent pay or started out with better motives, then connect with the greater source that your profession originated in—

the heart of a compassionate Papa. All work that is disconnected from God is ultimately hollow and draining. We were made to be an extension of our God. Jesus was God's light on earth,[7] and so are we. In Jesus' first public message, known as The Sermon on the Mount (simply because He was sitting on a hill when He shared it), He spoke to those gathered around Him and said, "You are the light of the world." [8] Just as Jesus came to dispel the darkness of the lies about who God is and who we are, He gave an invitation to all to represent God's true heart in the earth through all areas of culture. He declared they were the light of the world created to shine and reflect all the colors of God—even before they knew of their need for eternal salvation that His death and resurrection from the dead would make available to them. The people Jesus spoke to did not yet know how to "get saved," but He was already telling them that they were called to be the light of the world and the salt of the earth.

Ultimately, if we can't sense that we are co-laboring with God in the profession we chose, it may be the wrong profession for us. Either we change our mentality and connect to His heart for where we are, or we must go and search for the area of His heart that He wants to express through us. We will never experience true fulfillment until we do and until we know what love looks like coming out of us.

Pastors are generally viewed as those who are called to help families in need. Though this is still true, the reality is that by the time pastors are brought into a family crisis, it may be too late. Usually government social agencies have already been involved, and the rejection issues have advanced so much, that pastors end up bringing more comfort than actual healing. That's why I would recommend that those with a heart to impact families work with government social agencies, counseling services, the legislative branch, and other alternatives rather than the traditional role of pas-

---

7   John 9:5
8   Matthew 5:14

tors in the context of churches. Regardless, if you have a heart to bring healing to the wounds of rejection, you are in fact recognized by God as a true "pastor" whether you carry this title or not. Yes, families should be able to find healing in churches, but we also need pastors in many additional structures of society as well. You may have always known you were called to be a pastor and tried to make it work out in a more typical church setting, but it didn't work for you. Maybe it's time to take another look at how your calling could bring the influence of heaven on the families of our generation. Papa God's color orange is needed everywhere.

THE HOPEFUL FUTURE FOR FAMILIES

The good news is that, in the end, Papa God is going to shine His true colors throughout our families. There will be breakthrough wisdom for family relationships that God will release through His sons and daughters who labor with Him. Important advances in understanding how to "rewire" the brain will continue to lead to great help for complex aberrant behaviors and addictions, as well as for more normal issues we tend to struggle with. We have already learned so much about the differences in the "hard drive" of males versus females. Anyone working toward improving communication between humans is working for Papa God. And as He is invited into our research, He will begin to provide even more understanding about core issues. We are about to receive such tremendous help from His blazing lamp that stands before His throne that we will ultimately model the healthiest societies ever seen in the history of planet earth. Where He is not invited in, society will continue to de-grade, not because He is angry with us or judging sin, but because He will never impose Himself. He wants true intimacy with us. Where He is invited in, we will begin to look like heaven's model of family.

INVITE HIM IN—AS PAPA

As we said in the previous chapter, we will use each line, one by one, of "The Lord's Prayer" to help you connect to a new personal perspective of God in a way that changes you. Why read a book if it doesn't impact you in a practical way, right? So to finish this chapter, we will begin with the first line of the prayer and then continue in each chapter with the next line.

Jesus began His model prayer with **"Our Father, who is in Heaven."** *So much healing and freedom is packed into this short statement. Jesus must have been aware that, for generations to come, the sons and daughters of God would pray this same prayer in every language through the happiest and saddest of times, from the lips of an innocent child to the last words of the guiltiest among us.*

Built into "The Lord's Prayer" is a tutorial for how to invite God into our lives and our culture. It starts with the fundamental truth that every heart needs to know in order to thrive—we have a Father. Our broken families have been a harbor for the lies of rejection, but the truth that God is our real Father eradicates that source of pain, if we will believe it.

Not only do our hearts need to know that we have a Father who loves and cares for us, but we need a sense of family too. So many are hurting because they not only didn't have parents, they also missed out on all the good that comes from being a part of a healthy family or household. Jesus specifically prayed OUR Father. When we pray like He taught us to pray, within the first two words, we speak the reality that God isn't just MY Father, but OUR Father. You and I have the same Father. We are one another's family. And Jesus is our brother. There is a household of God and of faith for those who believe, and it reaches far beyond any temple, church, mosque, or cathedral. We may not be perfect, but we are to Him. And like all good sons and daughters, we will eventually grow up to be just like our Papa when we finally realize what He is really like. Evidently, He will also trust us for all of eternity to share in the family business! I can't wait to see what that's all about.

Jesus also prayed to the One "who is in heaven." After all we have talk-
ed about in this chapter—how our natural families pale in comparison to
what we needed and were meant to have—it's refreshing to remember that
this Father, our real Father who can meet our need for love and acceptance,
is the One who is in heaven. He exists. He is real. We know where He is, and
therefore we have access to Him and all we need from Him.

Another really cool thing about this prayer is that, when we say it out
loud, it has the potential to literally rewire our brain. Neuroscientists have
proven that when your brain hears your voice speak something out loud,
it creates a new pathway for thought to travel on in the brain. Something
about our voice causes a chemical response that only happens when we hear
ourselves speak. And when that chemical response happens, the neurons
that thoughts travel on in the brain connect, forming new pathways of
thought. The more you say something, the more you think it; and the more
traveled that pathway of thought is, the easier that way of thinking becomes.
It's the basic idea behind developing habits. It is also proven that up until
around the age of puberty, when certain hormones kick in, the voice of our
authority figures create the same neurological responses in us. So here's
the good news: if you were told painful things in your childhood and you
subsequently struggle with certain issues as an adult, God has built into
this prayer the remedy for your rejection. When you speak this truth out
loud, "Our Father, who is in heaven," you are giving your heart permission
to believe that your real Father is in heaven and that what He thinks, feels,
and says about you is what really matters. You are establishing in yourself
the reality that you are part of the family of God, even if your temporary
family let you down.

If you aren't sure what He thinks about you, just ask Him. He created you
with the ability to perceive His voice in all the ways that He speaks.[9] Most
importantly, don't forget to invite Him in, wherever and whenever you need
a Papa. He is happy to be to you what you may have never gotten from your

---

9   If you want to learn more about how to recognize when and how God speaks to us, you
can go to our website and order the DVD series and workbook called "Hearing God."

mom or dad. He can handle whatever you bring Him. Start with being honest with Him, even if you're angry. But don't stop there. Ask Him all the hard questions and expect responses. Tell Him how you need His acceptance and love to heal your rejection. Ask Him to look beyond your walls of protection and touch your heart like only He can. Ask Him to be your **strength,** *your* **Papa.**

CHAPTER FOUR

REDEEMER: The Color of Honor
THE SOLUTION FOR OUR RELIGIONS

As much as religion seems to divide us, religion is possibly the greatest proof of how much we all have in common. And what we have in common is far more than our differences—a desperation to know God and be free from the walls that we have built that keep us from feeling the love and acceptance we instinctively crave from Him.

Judaism, Islam, Christianity, Buddhism, Confucianism, Hinduism, Bahai, Sikhism, Taoism, Jainism, Shinto, and Zoroastrianism—this is just the beginning of a long list of religions of the world. Perhaps there are as many religions as there have been individual people. We all have our own way of relating or not relating to God, even in the context of a specific faith we may have been taught. Some religions even say that there are many ways to God. As a Christian, I (Elizabeth) would say there are many personal journeys but only one way. Whatever your opinion is of religion, surely we can agree that eventually, our personal journeys lead us to the need and desire for a relationship with something and someone greater than ourselves. Someone who understands and can make sense of all that we cannot. Someone who was intentional with our reason for existing and equally as intentional with whatever comes next. Something stronger than us, wiser, and a refuge from whatever it is that seems to always conspire against us.

Religion is a tricky subject, because like all truth, it is held in the tension of two opposing thoughts. Religion is worth living for and dying for—the freedom for humans to choose for themselves if, who, or what they will worship. On the other hand, religion is also the biggest enemy to love, which is the very essence of who God is. In the subtitle of this chapter, like all the other chapters, we speak of the solution for one of the seven primary areas of our cultures. Well, the solution for our religions, is NO religion. Freedom of religion, yes. But what about freedom **from** religion and freedom of **relationship**? We are born with the right to have our own beliefs or religion, but we are not truly free until we realize that religion is bondage if it does not bring us into a relationship with God Himself rather than a relationship with rules.

As a reminder, we're expanding our perception of who God really is and learning to see Him as the God of all of life, who has the solution and better ways for every area of culture. Think about it: if there is a God, then He Himself is indeed the solution for everything that isn't right. Religion, as opposed to simply a personal healthy relationship with God, has been the source of many of history's most savage wars. Religion is the cause of millions of deaths across generations. There is something not right about religion—something quite wrong, and a huge need for improving, just like other areas of culture. Could God be the answer to our problem of religion? Is there an aspect of God Himself that is the solution we need for the problems of religion? Yep.

LOVE DISPLAYED AS HONOR

What does religion look like when the real God is actually in it? If you aren't so sure about Christianity, don't worry, I am not about to say that Christianity is the answer for the problems of religion. Many who have walked away from religion have done so because of their experiences with Christians. God is not hoping we all convert to a religion called Christianity. He simply wants a relationship with us and sent His son Jesus Christ to heal *our relationship with Himself. But more on that later. God is love, so what does love look like in this area or sector of our culture?* **In the context of** *religion,* **love looks like** *honor. And honor is far from simply following rules, laws, and behaving right out of obligation. Honor is showing respect from a heart that is impacted by what or whom it is interacting with. When we say, "I am honored to meet you," we are communicating how privileged we feel. It's supposed to be a response that is heartfelt and genuine. When religion is true worship that is birthed out of love and not performance, then honor is restored to a nation's culture through whatever religions are present. A sense of awe and wonder of how amazing God is can bring real relationship and overtake the false religions we have settled for.*

God established the law of nature that causes rainbows to appear in order to remind Himself and us of His true heart for us, beyond the lies of this earthly perspective. **Blue** *is the color of* **redemption** *and we use it to refer to the sector or structure of society called* **religion.** *So what does* **blue** *tell us about God? The color blue is quite universal in the thoughts it triggers in us—thoughts of the vast ocean and sky and the awe they inspire. When we think of God as Creator, it causes our hearts to worship or be in awe and honor Him. Honor is reverence, value, and a deep respect.[1] Many of us have an easier time accessing a sense of God and worship of Him in the beauty of the outdoors, outside the four walls of a church, temple, cathedral, or mosque. False religion locks us and our perspective of God into a building, but relationship sees a God that cannot be contained in the boxes human beings create. True worship is a childlike response to something that moves us rather than a ritual or obligation to fulfill an expectation. Honor is a response to love—to God, who is love. A great real-life example of honor is seen in the United States Army Medal of Honor. It is presented to families of soldiers or the soldiers themselves who have risked their lives in action above and beyond the call of duty. You could say they have been moved to action by love rather than simply by what is expected of them. The Medal of Honor, interestingly, has been typically blue in its design throughout the years that it has been awarded.*

---

1   New Oxford American Dictionary

*Whatever calls itself love must ultimately be like its source, God. God evokes honor, that sense of worship and respect, from us because that's who He is as well. He has shown us honor by loving us even when we don't deserve it based on how we act or respond to Him. His love and honor of us is unconditional. So we **give** Him honor and He **is** honor. It's kind of like telling a judge, "Your Honor, I honor you." We are made in His image as those who are created both to give and receive honor. So if we claim to have religion and a relationship with God, then our love and actions must be infused with honor. Otherwise, it's false religion and far from the real God.*

Pure and undefiled religion is full of love expressed as honor. When you honor or respect someone, you are treating them as someone of value and worth, whether or not you think they deserve it. You give honor because you have a core value for honor. If a religion does not carry in its expression honor—of not only God, but women, all races, all classes, and basically all humans—then it is most certainly a false religion, far less than God's original invitation to us, His sons and daughters. Even if we never all agree on what kind of relationship with God is real, what would happen if we all embraced love and honor of all people as fundamental to religion? Now that would be peace on earth. When you are an honorable person, you do not murder in the name of God. When you truly honor God, you honor those He created, whether you agree with them or not.

Blue, being one of the seven colors of love that we are looking at, speaks to us about God as **Redeemer**, the One who has given us our lives back so that we could fully live and know Him in all the ways He shows up in life. This is the face of God that we Christians have promoted perhaps more than any other. As grateful as I (Johnny) am for God as my Redeemer, He is not simply one identity we respond to. He is multifaceted in who He is, and we must learn to see Him and relate to Him in this way. Though it may be new for many, this should not seem strange because we are similarly made in His multifaceted image.

One description alone does not suffice to describe each of us as individuals. Even when someone is called a God-fearing person, it's usually just describing one aspect of who they are. If someone were to describe me to others, I would hope they would have something to say that goes beyond that—God-fearing, but also a man who loves his family, enjoys sports, is interested in learning new things, and follows government, media, and entertainment, ultimately greatly interested in all areas of life. This is not being distracted **from** God, this is being distracted by or drawn **into** God.

I grew up around some well-meaning, religious people who erroneously thought that attention to normal aspects of life and culture were distractions from what really mattered in life—God. Unfortunately, many Christian leaders today live as if they believe that too. They believe that because God is mainly concerned with the state of our heart for eternity, anything that doesn't connect directly to someone getting saved is a distraction from what really matters. Because of that, most followers of God have cared most about representing Him only as Redeemer, even though He is additionally all the other colors of the rainbow. It really is hard to argue with the fact that this aspect of Him is the most important one, but overemphasizing this aspect comes from a limited perspective.

Maybe because of that, no matter where you stand on earth, the color of the sky is always some shade of blue. It is the backdrop of everything. Behind every cloud and every rainbow there's blue sky. He is the God of all life, but He grafted Himself into our personal lives through what Jesus did on the cross. He continues to be with us palpably through the Holy Spirit. The Holy Spirit is called the Spirit of Truth, and truth is represented by blue. You've heard of the expression "true blue." When you fly over the oceans, you see blue. When you look up into the heavens you see blue. God our Redeemer reveals Himself everywhere. In the same way that you can't appreciate a colorful sunset apart from the blue sky that it sinks into, one cannot embrace the God of all of life apart from God as Redeemer of our souls.

THE LIE:
WE HAVE TO WORK HARD AND BE GOOD
IN ORDER TO KNOW GOD

Religion, including Christianity, tends to create a feeling in us that we are not pleasing to God and that we must earn His approval. Religion reminds us of how distant we are from God and how much we need to do in order to know Him. It's true that there are things that can separate us from Him if not dealt with, but trying to earn His approval isn't the solution. When we settle for religion instead of relationship, the pressure is clearly on us to somehow be good enough and holy enough to be close to Him and secure for ourselves some kind of place in His presence.

The difference between the God of the Bible and all other religions is that Jesus Christ is the solid evidence that God was willing to do what we couldn't do for ourselves. He not only created a set of standards to help us individually and collectively see our need for His redemption, but He Himself did exactly what needed to be done in order for us to know Him. That is all He ever really wanted and the reason He created humanity to begin with—to have an intimate relationship with us where we know Him just like He knows us—the real Him and not the one we have wrongly perceived.

There isn't one person who was ever born who didn't have a longing to be close to their dad in a way that was far more than how it actually worked out. We have all known that disappointment because only a perfect God could fulfill that desire. That desire is proof of what we were originally created to have with our Heavenly Father. But that kind of intimacy, as we have said, requires free will and choice, along with an opportunity for trust that can then produce intimacy.

A desire for intimacy also requires the awareness of a need for relationship to be restored and the realization that you cannot do that yourself. Many people wake up to their desire for relationship with God, but they become deceived by the counterfeit of false religion and get stuck trying to restore the relationship through working hard and trying to be good. They find a religion that has a list of requirements they feel and hope they can somehow measure up to. Muslims, Jews, Buddhists, and even Christians all have their list of requirements. We are all wired similarly, so the enemy lures us with the same strategy, but with different criteria. We all have different personalities and levels of resolve, but most eventually hit that burnout point where we get frustrated because we simply cannot perform and are tired of feeling bad about our inability to be whatever it is we were taught God needs us to be.

Again, Satan has the one basic lie that he repackages in many ways to lead us into the cycle of trying to earn love that has been given freely by a good Papa. Does he have you stuck in a game of religion? Even Christians fall into this deception. We want so badly to feel like we have value and worth, that we try to behave in a way that makes us feel like God could be happy with us. The truth is, none of us will ever sense the true worth and value that we have from religion. Knowing how loved and valued we are only comes out of relationship, and relationship only comes through what God sent His Son Jesus to do for us. The most healing and freeing thing we can realize is that we already have the very value that we crave. It was given to us long before we awaken to a relationship with God, before we even drew our first breath.

As we will unfold in the rest of this chapter, Jesus is the proof of the love and worth we have in God's eyes before we ever come to know Him or His ways. The way we learn to act and behave after we come into relationship with Him is meant to be a response, not a requirement, to having been redeemed.

HOW DOES THIS LIE ABOUT GOD PLAY OUT IN CULTURE?

If religion is work and performance, then God is a tyrant and taskmaster who pushes us to carry an impossible workload. When we wrongly perceive Him as a demanding, needy being, we are basically left to respond in one of three ways: try to work hard enough to appease Him, stay bitter and angry with Him for putting us in that position, or, as a subtle form of rebellion against such apparent cruelty, roll over and pretend He doesn't exist. I believe most who have lived long enough have responded in each way at some point, which has created quite an ongoing collective turmoil in society.

In the first choice, if we choose to work hard and try to somehow measure up, it leaves us stuck in a cycle of almost being able to pull it off and then failing miserably. That cycle then causes us to feel full of shame and a sense of inadequacy. When we feel insecure and bad about ourselves, we are quick to react, defend, and blame-shift whenever we sense our true self is being judged. These are usually the most religious among us. I (Elizabeth) know because I have been one who was enslaved to that cycle. It wasn't until I finally gave up on religion and found an intimate relationship with God that I felt truly free. Those who live under this version of religion ultimately experience shame that slowly steals their life.

In the second scenario, if we believe God demands unattainable standards, then over time we become resentful. We continue to keep some form of relationship to God or religion, but at a safe distance. We choose a level of interaction that we can maintain without too much sacrifice. The assumption is that if we got too close, then we might have to be honest with ourselves and God about our anger, and that somehow feels disrespectful to the One we know in theory created us and loves us. So when we respond to this incorrect concept of God, we tend to go through the motions of our particular religion but live distantly from Him. We grow bitter because we know in our heart of hearts we were created to feel His love and acceptance, and we don't. We try to fill our lives with other distractions, some good and some not; but either way, the grief of not having the intimacy we were created for slowly kills us.

Lastly, more and more people seem to be choosing to simply opt out of the God-game. Either the little they know of it has no appeal, or what they have studied or seen leaves them with quite a distaste for it. If you perceive God or religion to be unreasonable in what it requires, or at least sub-consciously, you simply refuse to believe in God at all. You can't afford to acknowledge a need for a God that is going to disappoint you. And it would be disappointing if most of our contrived versions of Him were true. At some point, it takes more faith to embrace a lie that says we have no real meaning for being here than it does to face the reality of hoping that there is a God who is as good as *we hope He is. Because we were made to have access to the Source of all we are craving, eventually the effort it takes to defend our unbelief slowly destroys us.*

Every nation across our globe has built into its overall culture our man-made versions of God or religion. No one religion has it right or is perfect, because all are influenced by imperfect people. By the way, that doesn't make God or His heart for us less than perfect. In our collective attempt to navigate our way to God, we establish our own standard of truth based on whatever seems right to us. The problem is that, like everything else, we filter what we think is right through our personal experiences and perceptions of those experiences. Truth, by its very definition, cannot be subjective. It has to be absolute. It is not a feeling or a fad that comes and goes with the whims of whatever generation is presently leading. God is truth, the very standard and unchanging reality that reality is based on, no matter what culture or nation you live in. Religion, like the other primary areas of culture that we are mentioning, is our response to Truth, to God Himself. Religion is not God but rather our response to who we perceive Him to be. No religion at all is equally our response to who we perceive God to be.

Many religious people live out of a lie that says we must work hard and be good (whatever our religion's description of good is) in order to know God. This lie permeates every nation and every area of each nation's culture. Governments, economies, education systems, families, and our forms of media and entertainment are greatly impacted by this deception. We make wars and threats over defending not just our right for freedom to choose religion but over our attempts to carry out what we think God expects of us. For example, some extreme Muslims wage what they are taught is a holy war against those who don't see their version of God the way they do. They believe they are pleasing God when they rid the world of those who break God's rules. Of course we as Christians would never do that, at least not anymore. We think it's somehow better to just judge and hate rather than kill those who aren't willing to work hard like we do to earn God's approval. (Ouch, did I say that?) We need to let the scales of this lie fall off all of our eyes in every nation and religion.

WHO IS GOD—AS REDEEMER?

"Redeem" means "to regain possession of by payment, ransom, or payment for the release of a prisoner." [2] A redeemer is "one who buys back or repurchases." [3] We all start off belonging to God. He created us, so we are His sons and daughters, even if we don't know we are or refuse to recognize that others are.

We all stray and find ourselves heading away from God. Satan and his demons use their influence to deceive us into following his ways or our own ways rather than God's. We become prisoners to Satan's lies and need rescuing from our self-dependence. Those of us who are parents have seen it played out in real time with our toddlers, even the cutest ones of all, who eventually prefer their own way over ours despite our intention to protect them. We also see it play out with our adolescents and teens who quickly learn to believe the lies that we as adults spend our adult years trying to unlearn.

Similarly, we all go astray like wandering sheep. It's interesting that the Bible describes us like sheep[4]—not evil, just prone to wandering from where they are protected and in need of being looked after. Our going astray always involves being in sin.

"Being in sin" is behaving in ways that grieve God's heart, not because He's easily offendable but because He loves us. All sin is bad for us whether we know it or not. "Not sinning" is not just about trying to please a demanding God. It's about doing what is actually best for us. The One who created us knows what is best for us—a novel concept. He also always has our ultimate good in mind.

Sin literally means "to miss the way or to miss the mark." It's basically anything we do or think that falls short of the original way God had planned for us. It was never meant to be a word that causes us to feel shame, just conviction. Shame is Satan's counterfeit for conviction. Shame makes you feel

---

2   New Oxford American Dictionary.
3   New Oxford American Dictionary
4   Isaiah 53:6

like you're a failure, but conviction that's appropriate and healthy causes you to recognize that you have failed so you can learn from it and do something about it.

God set things up in such a way that we can know, from outside and within, when we sin—when we are missing His better way for us. He set us up to be able to succeed in our pursuit of a relationship with Himself. Internally, God created each of us with a conscience so that we could, with His help, deal with anything that keeps us from living a life that is healthy in every way, with nothing between Him and us. He wants our relationship with Him to be free from the things that make us feel shame so we can always run to Him as our source for whatever we need. Externally, through the Bible, God also gave us an idea of the kinds of things that bring that sense of shame, separation, and a slow death to the freedom He wants us all to live in.

Surely you have heard the Biblical and historical account of how an ordinary man named Moses received the 10 commandments. He was invited by God to meet with Him in the mountains. During that time, the God of all creation showed His continued desire for relationship by speaking face to face with Moses so he could document God's laws or standards of how to live the best life for us and for our communities. If you can, rid your memory of the fake-looking movie scenes of a guy with long, white hair and a deep-voiced God who only spoke in "thees and thous," and let the reality of it sink in. God wants us to know the keys to life. Jesus later told us that the reason God gave us that list of do's and don'ts was not so that we could work hard to keep the rules but to show us that it was impossible. He wanted us to see our need to receive Him as our righteousness.[5]

Righteousness is simply when something or someone is in right standing with God. Right standing with God is when we are close to Him rather than distant from Him. The purpose of the commandments or laws was ultimately to restore us to Himself, not to make us work hard so we could please some distant God. We don't wish to offend anyone who has chosen to worship a manmade idol, whether it's the Catholic statues of Jesus or Mary, the golden

---

5   Galatians 2:16; 3:10-13, 22-25; Romans 3:9-26; 8:1-4; 2 Corinthians 5:21.

Buddha, or Indian shrines that sit and wait for little tokens to be laid before them, but how in the world can anyone maintain an allegiance to a man-made object that doesn't interact with you? How we settle for a version of some distant god who is like the mafia boss that must be paid off and appeased! Christians do it too. We want God, but somehow we are easily deceived into thinking we can perform to get Him. So we create our version of performance that is difficult enough to be some level of sacrifice but still attainable. How's that working for us?! God loved us so much that He gave us an impossible list so we would try, fail, and come running to Him for relationship rather than settle for religion that leaves us exhausted from futile efforts.

God's laws produced, and still do, a dividing line within our hearts. Do we want relationship or religion? They lead all of us, if we allow them, to humility and a realization that what we really want, we cannot earn. That humility is the very thing we must have in order to recognize that Jesus, as ordinary as He seemed to be when He walked the earth, was indeed the answer to our desire for closeness to God. As much as I (Elizabeth) love my Jewish brothers and sisters, I must point out that, unfortunately, many of their religious leaders in the days of Jesus were so set on working hard at keeping those laws, they couldn't recognize Jesus for who He really was and what He came to do for them. They were too addicted to the pain medicine to trade it in for the real cure. Jesus came to relieve them, and all of us, from the propensity we have to earn God's love when it's impossible.

In our humanity, there is something in all of us that at least subconsciously believes that if God were to do something really important, He would do it in a way that we would easily recognize it. The most influential people of the time when Jesus lived thought just like we do—that if Jesus was really from God and was His Son, He would surely show up just how we would expect Him to show up. That didn't happen then, and it still doesn't because this God is humble. When He shows up, it's with humility, and it takes humility to see Him.

So who is God as Redeemer? The Bible, when read through the lens of seeing Him being a good God who desires us to be close to Him, paints an amazing picture of Him as our Redeemer. It's the story of the One who ransomed *us from religion and everything that keeps us distant from God. The commandments of the Old Testament (the time period from creation until Jesus' birth), were a big part of what Jesus taught about later in the New Testament (the second part of the Bible). Jesus reminded us that He came to fulfill the law that God had given to Moses. "Fulfill" means to bring to completion or satisfy. Jesus satisfied the commandments of God so we could have the benefits of them in our lives without having to perfectly fulfill them ourselves. Jesus, being fully God but limited to our earthly perspectives, lived the only perfect life that has ever been lived. He then was raised from the dead by God after being crucified as our sacrifice on a cross in order to defeat the last thing we are incapable of defeating—death. Our Redeemer cares about our lives now **and** in the hereafter. We have been redeemed from sin and from death. Can your religion do that?*

If the laws of God were meant to connect us with our need for a Redeemer, then should we still work on our behavior? Yes, once we own the fact that we can't and don't have to make ourselves close to God because Jesus did it for us. We can't earn God's favor, but we still want to have a life that is full of true freedom, right? For example, when God tells us not to lie, it's not so we will please Him but because lying actually degrades who we are. It makes our words lose power and effectiveness and ultimately leaves us outside of the circle of anyone's trust. In His better way of doing everything, He understands how our word is all we have and honesty is our way of maintaining that.

God tells us "Don't steal," not just so we don't offend Him, but again because of how it degrades our spirit. A spirit that feels like it has to steal in order to be fulfilled is a spirit disconnected from One who is the Source of all we could possibly need. Stealing is a sign that our internal hard drive is beginning to burn out. Of course, it's obviously unjust toward the one being stolen from. Even in this we see His heart toward us as humans. By telling **us** not to steal, He is also saying, "I don't want you to have things stolen from **you**."

When God says, "Don't commit adultery," He wants us to obey for very practical reasons other than just honoring Him—which admittedly should be enough. He doesn't want us committing adultery because it's an instrument of murder against our families. Every time someone commits adultery, they are in fact bringing death to whatever family that they have. If you cheat on your spouse, you are essentially killing your marriage and your family unit. The repercussions of adultery are felt beyond the marriage and family and into the extended family. Ditto for the other party involved in the adultery. The fruit of adultery has never been and never will be good. It will always end in some kind of serious pain and damage. Even if you never get caught and the damage seems limited, you will have been guilty of stealing trust from your mate. Whatever part of your heart you have given the other party, you are withholding from your spouse. There's no need to belabor this point because there is almost universal understanding that adultery goes beyond offending God to being extremely damaging to everyone even remotely connected.

What about premarital sex? How can it be bad for two people in love to be physically intimate? It isn't, as long as those two people will enter into a lifelong covenant of commitment before God first. If you already recognize adultery as damaging, sex before marriage is just pre-adultery. Most adulterers will also have been immoral before marriage. Someone who is willing to trample over the covenant of marriage is usually someone who never respected covenant to begin with. Both are just profound manifestations of selfishness. I want what I want when I want it—even if God knows how everything will function best.

Can anyone argue that a society that innately followed the 10 commandments would be the most healthy society? It does get complicated when we try to figure out who would enforce morality, but I don't think any reasonable human being thinks a lying, cheating, sexually promiscuous society is a healthy foundation for raising a child in.

God has given us all the ingredients for having a successful and blessed life. He gives us rules so we don't hurt ourselves with the good things He gives us. We don't let our infants play with fire at all, and we let our teens do so only under strict guidelines and supervision, even though fire is good in the right context. When we're older, we have free access to matches and lighters, but we use utmost care because fire can create great damage. Similarly, God gives us the great gift of sex. When we're young, it is not to be used at all, and even when older we do so following great safety guidelines. As with fire, the guidelines by parents are not an attempt to be control freaks. God has a reason for everything He asks of us. For every "no" He gives us, there's a good reason other than "Because I said so." There is a "why" to everything, but as with our kids, it's good for us to be okay with not understanding sometimes and choosing to trust. God is the most reasonable person in the universe.

So sin is doing things our way instead of God's way. Lying, cheating, stealing, having sex outside of marriage, and wanting what doesn't belong to us are just examples of behaviors that are not like His character or nature. All visible sins are hatched in the mind and spirit. This means that the reason we are prone to commit all these sins is because something underneath that behavior is also wrong. There is a deeper root issue that we eventually act out of. If you have never lied, never stolen, never cheated, never lusted, never coveted, nor ever **thought** of doing any of these, then you do not need a Redeemer. You can have full access to God based on your good core and behavior. You are so like Him that you don't have to feel intimidated by His intense perfection and holiness. However, if in fact you have recognized that not everything you have done and thought is something you are proud of, then maybe you don't want to casually saunter up to God or to His Heaven. The bottom line is, we all need a Redeemer God.

The Bible says that God is a consuming fire. Picture Him as the Sun, which is a ball of fire. It represents the purity of God's emotions and intentions toward us. If you could be pure in these areas, you too could be like the Sun and freely interact with Him with no fear of being burned up. Fire is never consumed by fire. Now picture every thought and deed of yours that you would not want others to see on YouTube. Every one of those is like dry wood and straw. The more of them you have, the more you are made out of these highly flammable materials. Now imagine trying to draw close to God or to His home if you are not like Him, equally pure and holy.

Holiness is not some part of God that needs us to behave because He likes to be demanding. If you got too close to the Sun and were killed by its fire, it would not be because the Sun is mad at you. The Sun is what it is, and unless we are like it, it consumes us simply because of its essence. In the same way, the holiness and perfection of God is His essence, and whatever is in us that's not like Him is consumed when we draw near to Him. The holiness of God doesn't kill us because God is mad with us but because, by its very nature, it consumes whatever is not holy also. If we have not exchanged our sin (the ways we are not like God) for Jesus' perfect ability to do things God's way, by faith, then the presence of God that we so desperately want and were created to live in will destroy us. This is why we need another way of access to His heart and to His home — the Redeemer God.

THE TRUTH:
WE NEED A REDEEMER IN ORDER TO KNOW GOD

The Bible explains that "everyone has sinned; we all fall short of God's glorious standard." [6] Have we convinced you that is true yet? Please contact us if you're the exception here so we can meet you! So let's assume the Bible probably knows what it's talking about when it says "**all** have sinned" and, therefore, we are all less than fireproof.

Scripture explains the redemption process with great clarity.

"Yet, God, with undeserved kindness, declares that we are righteous. He did this through Christ Jesus when He freed us from the penalty of our sins. For God presented Jesus as the

---

6   Romans 3:23 New Living Translation

sacrifice for sin. People are made right with God when they believe that Jesus sacrificed His life shedding His blood. This sacrifice shows that God was being fair when he held back and did not punish those who sinned in times past."[7]

Wow, what an amazing God! He makes what Jesus did on the cross to have a retroactive effect. Even Goliath (the giant that David killed with just a slingshot), who had been dead and gone a long time when Jesus gave His life, was given the opportunity to come into right standing with God. He could have said, "I get it. I'm sorry for the wicked way I lived. I am sorry for calling your buddy David all those bad names. I claim this privilege for myself and believe that what Jesus did on the cross extends to even me." Can you imagine our surprise if we find Goliath in Heaven? Don't worry, all the bullying will be out of his system. When you come into Heaven in Jesus' robes of righteousness, everything that was impure burns up between the earth and heaven. Your spirit and soul gets chiseled down to what it was created to be, the real you.

Continuing with Goliath as an example, I'm sure he was created with a good personality. He was thought up originally in the heart of God, and what God does is good. However his likely dysfunctional family life, connected to the fact that they worshipped demons, was not so good for his development, and let's just say he strayed. Now to allow someone as mean as Goliath to have retroactive access into Heaven can't come cheaply. This requires more than a snap of the fingers. There's a price to pay that only God Himself could pay.

Only righteous blood could satisfy the need for holiness that can withstand closeness to the One who is holy. So God the Son willingly came to earth and became man because a human being's sacrifice is what was required for the redemption price of humanity to be satisfied. Jesus lived until He was 30, the age of maturity in the Jewish

---

7   Romans 3:24-25 New Living Translation

culture, never having manifested a thought or an action that was in contradiction to God the Father. People mistakenly think Jews killed Jesus, when in reality He willingly gave Himself as the price to be paid so all humans could vicariously have access to God and Heaven. Wow! There is a reason you go to Hell if you turn that down. For God to allow Himself to be crucified by His own children is no small thing. Many parents may experience that symbolically perhaps, but there is nothing like what Jesus went through. Watch Mel Gibson's movie "The Passion of Christ" to get a taste of what that felt like. That movie did me in; it's impossible to watch it without sensing the depth of Jesus' sacrifice.

One of the most famous songs ever sung says it best. "Amazing grace, how sweet the sound, that saved a wretch like me. I once was lost, but now I'm found, was blind, but now I see." Grace is receiving the favor of God without having to earn it. Truly His grace is amazing because it's what saves us from ourselves and opens our eyes to see how good He really is. When we stop busying ourselves from either working to earn His love or running from the shame we feel by falling short of trying to earn it, we have that sense that we have finally been found. We don't have to behave perfectly or think perfectly to be made right with God. He expects less than perfection from us. He says that if we will just believe that Jesus sacrificed His life on our behalf, we can be as close to Him as we choose to be and experience true intimacy, through God as our Redeemer.

If you have never acknowledged your need for redemption through Jesus, why not do it now? It's profoundly simple. If you believe that Jesus Christ is the Son of God who was sent to show us that our Papa loves us and is willing to redeem us, then you can receive the righteousness Jesus lived and be in right standing with God.[8] As you do this from the sincerity of your heart, your spirit will actually experience a rebirth,[9] and at this very moment your name will be written

---

8   Romans 3:26
9   John 3:3

in a massive real book in Heaven called "The Book of Life." [10] These are the official records of Heaven that gain you access into Heaven when you die. It might sound a little strange or hokey to think of a book of names, but would you want to serve a God who doesn't care enough to document how important you and your decisions are?

The Bible explains that if you confess with your mouth that Jesus is your Lord, meaning you recognize that you want to live for Him and not yourself, and believe in your heart that God raised Him from the dead, you will be saved or redeemed. Believing with your heart that Jesus has paid His life so you can be in right standing with God, and then declaring it with your own mouth, will begin a relationship with God that is real and will last for eternity. God wanted to make sure we understood that although we each have our own journey to discovering intimacy with Him, there is only one way to Him, and that is through receiving the One, Jesus, whom He sent to redeem or purchase us back from the deception of His enemy. When you declare Jesus as your Savior, or Redeemer, you are undoing the lies Satan perpetrated against our Papa's correct reputation from the beginning of creation. You are coming out of agreement with lies that present Him as less than who He really is. You are acknowledging the truth. And the truth is, you and I exist to know the real God, to make the real God known, and to learn to love Him, ourselves, and one another. Scripture also tells us that whoever believes in Christ Jesus will not be put to shame, and whoever calls out to Him, will be saved from everything we need to be saved from.[11]

You can read the following as your new confession of faith, if you have been so convinced in your heart.

"Jesus, I accept what you did on the cross as the substitutionary price for me so I could have full access to God and to Heaven. I acknowledge that I have sinned and am prone to sinning and do not on my own merit deserve this gift of grace. However,

---

10 Revelation 20:15
11 Romans 10:9-13

I embrace the humility of my lack, and with great gratitude I embrace you as God my Papa and Redeemer. Now please fill me with your Holy Spirit so my actions will begin to fall more in line with how You think and act. Amen."

By the way, the word Amen is not just some ritualistic religious word. It means "so be it" or "may it be fulfilled." When you say it at the end of your prayer or conversation with God, you are simply stating "Let it be!"

If you never made a declaration of your personal relationship with God through Jesus before, this is a historical day for you, whether you feel it or not. The "Book of Life" in Heaven will note this very time and this very date as your moment of new birth.

Ask God to help you connect with others who have found true intimacy with God. In an ideal world, you could simply find a Christian church (those who are followers of Christ) and know exactly the kind of people you are connecting with. There are many safe ones, but not all are a healthy expression of God. The same Holy Spirit (that part of God that speaks to our hearts and leads us into truth) who led you to this moment, is well able to lead you to a safe place for you to grow.

THERE IS ONE ENEMY IN THE WAR OVER RELIGION

We have talked about Satan, the enemy of God, and his hatred for God being so great that he has lashed out at God's creation because he knew he couldn't touch God Himself. If you have been alive very long, you know how good Satan is at being evil. If he can't get us to ruin our lives or other people's lives by leading us into believing or doing the wrong thing, then he gets behind us and pushes us too far in believing and doing the right thing. He saw our tendency as humans to reach out to our Creator for relationship and pushed us past the simplicity of true intimacy and into religion. In essence, Satan took our right to have a real relationship with our Father and deceived us into exchanging it for religion based on knowing principles rather than the freedom to know God Himself. Like every other good thing God has offered us, Satan offers a counterfeit. Religion, by definition, is a way of belief or worship. False religion is a set of rules or a system to follow in order to appease God. True religion is relationship, trust, and intimacy with God.

There is one enemy in the war over religion. Any religion that teaches its followers to look at anyone other than Satan himself as the enemy is a false religion. Because humans are the common denominator of all religions, you can be sure that all religions are guilty of pointing fingers at other people as the enemy rather than at the true source of all darkness. Yes, we can align ourselves knowingly or unknowingly with that one enemy, but ultimately even the most evil person on the planet is not the enemy but simply his pawn.

We discussed God as being three in one and the fact that we are made in His image. So we are also three in one—one person, but made up of a spirit, soul, and body. Of course our body is that part of us that eventually dies, but our spirit is that part of us that will either live for all of eternity with God or experience eternal death without God. Jesus said, *"God so loved the world that He gave His only Son, that whoever believes in Him would not die, but have eternal life."* [12] The death being described here is eternal death. The color blue that surrounds us in nature is meant to connect us to the reality of eternity.

Sometime just for curiosity's sake, do a search on YouTube of people who have had "life after death experiences." If you aren't convinced that we continue to exist once we die, then you will be. You'll find stories of many who suffered different kinds of deaths and were resuscitated, allowing them to come back and tell their obviously genuine encounters with heaven and hell. For someone who has had one of those experiences, it is impossible to convince them that there is no heaven or hell.

I (Elizabeth) like to think of this life like this—just like a baby is in the womb for nine months for the purpose of eventually being birthed into this

---

12 John 3:16

realm, we too are being prepared in this life for the purpose of being birthed into the realm of eternity. Just like a baby is fully alive in the womb but only somewhat able to comprehend its surroundings, so we too are fully alive in our spirits but not as able to comprehend as we one day will be able to. Just because that baby can't fully appreciate what it is being prepared to be birthed into doesn't mean that its soon-to-be home isn't real. Just because we cannot fully explain the mystery of the eternal spirit realm that we are going to one day be birthed into does not mean it is not very real.

Jesus taught that you can know some aspects of God well enough to do many things in His name but live outside of His laws and end up in Hell, eternally separated from Him.[13] Again, the point is not to work hard to keep His commands, but to realize you can't, accept Jesus as the One who did it for you, and embrace His laws as a loving Papa's better ways instead of your own.

There is a real Heaven, and there is a real Hell. Our Papa really doesn't want anyone to spend eternity in Hell. He has an intense and desperate desire that you would choose to spend all of eternity in the presence of His heart of love for you. Though I (Johnny) have a significant distaste for evangelists' messages that only value God's afterlife benefits, these are benefits that we all must have. This human life span is but a drop in the bucket compared to eternity, and we therefore need to make our eternal state secure.

The Bible, as well as stories from people's experiences, explain that Hell is very real and extremely horrible—worse than our greatest nightmare or scariest horror movie. Evidently Hell is endless pain and torment with all senses being continually defiled. It has a nauseating stench, the sounds are hideous, it is visually grotesque, and all emotions are saturated with hopelessness and despair. The only laughter is the sadistic laughs of demons torturing human souls. Every thought is torture with a constant recycling of fear, regret, foreboding, and panic. As opposed to life here on earth, all that you fear

---

13 Matthew 7:21-23

in Hell really is happening or going to happen. It's not just paranoia that you can talk yourself out of. It's your new reality. And there's no Xanax in Hell. No alcohol, no over-the-counter drugs, no cocaine, no heroine, no marijuana. There will be no help in handling the agony of this reality. Additionally, whoever ends up in Hell will be continually reminded of every time they refused God as their Redeemer. You may live eternally chained to the idol or activity you wouldn't give up in order to accept a living relationship with God. You will know depths of hopelessness that we can't even comprehend. Hell is hell, and I don't wish it on anyone. Neither does our Papa.

If your immediate reaction to this is to wonder how a good God could do something so severe, you need to understand that the choice of Hell is ours, not God's. We are all born with the gift of free will, and God will give everyone of us multiple opportunities to choose intimacy with Him. And remember, you can't have intimacy with Him apart from trusting Him. You can't trust Him if you aren't ever presented the need to have to trust Him, and you don't need to trust something or someone that you completely understand and contains no mystery.

God is just, so He will not send any to Hell who have not had a reasonable chance to make a choice. Because of that, no infant or child can ever be sent to Hell. They haven't had reasonable opportunity to make a choice about God. God is so fair that we need not worry about everyone being given a choice. He will give repeat opportunities for choosing Him. But no one ever knows when he or she has just received their last opportunity.

Hell is awful because it is the antithesis of everything good—the extreme opposite of the presence of our Papa and Redeemer, who is the source of everything good. Whereas Heaven will be far beyond our wildest dreams in a positive way, Hell will be worse than our worst nightmare. To reject a God who is this good, the source of light itself, is to leave yourself with the only remaining option—living with the very source of darkness and lies, Satan, the enemy of God.

HOW CAN WE COOPERATE WITH GOD AS REDEEMER
IN RESTORING HONOR TO RELIGION?

Your personal story, called your testimony, is your greatest instrument of collaboration with God the Redeemer. To the degree you have had a genuine encounter with God the Redeemer, to that degree you become an effective carrier of the good news of who He is and His heart for His sons and daughters. All religions have some good ideas and some good doctrines and disciplines. However, only through Christ is eternal salvation made a viable option for you. Most other religions carry good ideas, comments, and suggestions. But at the end of the day, they leave you going to sleep every night in doubt about your eternal future. You wonder, was I good enough today? If God judged by the curve, you might get into Heaven with a few righteous acts and with not having committed any horrible sins yourself. But He doesn't. Unfortunately, the standard is God Himself.

The amazing thing about the real God, as we have talked about, is that He set the standard and then fulfilled it for us because He so badly wants us to know His true heart for us. He not only wants us to know what it's like to be close to Him, but He wants us to be close to Him forever.

We co-labor with God the Redeemer as we live and tell about the incredible news of salvation. As we're able to be used by God to connect others to Him through faith in Jesus, we greatly please the heart of our Redeemer. Like any good Papa, He wants His children to know the truth of what He feels about them and that He has done what it takes so we can know and be close to Him. He will never force Himself on any of us, but He makes the truth available to us when we are genuinely hungry for it. Those who know Him will do the same.

If you remember, honor is that genuine sense of awe and worship provoked in our hearts by a correct perspective of God. So when we talk about restoring honor to religion, we're speaking of restoring an authentic response to seeing the real God, not a pressure to perform and measure up to a standard that may or may not even be the standard God has given us. What will move our hearts to the wonder of who He is more than seeing Him as He really is in the many ways He displays His love? *He's the Rainbow God of all of life who not only offers eternal life but has a most fascinating mission and purpose for us here on earth. That mission is first to get to know this real God of all colors, and then, part two, to make Him known—to see Him re-imaged and re-presented in every area of life.*

Every re-imaging of God is a manifestation of His love, and love is the essence of our mission. His love is multifaceted and multidimensional, and there is a unique manifestation of love for each area of society. We have delved into what His love looks like in family and now in religion, and will continue in the next chapters to see His love as another way in Government, Media, Education, Economy, and even what it looks like in Arts and Entertainment—the seven dimensions of love. Ultimately we restore honor to religion when we embrace the reality that we have been redeemed in order that we can know Him and His love in all of life, and not just in the context of religion.

THE HOPEFUL FUTURE FOR RELIGION

God is about to reveal Himself as never before to a whole generation of broken, hurting people. His "glowing with Jesus" sons and daughters will rise up as never before, and they will volunteer to penetrate the darkest recesses of the planet with the light of His love. This generation will manifest such an attractive God that millions upon millions will choose intimacy with the real God instead of settling for religious rituals. They will embrace the mission of co-laboring with Him in every area of society, discovering what love looks like in all of culture, outside the walls of a church building. God is about to shake everything so that what is left standing is real. False religions, even churches, that are not true representations of Himself will eventually crumble. He will showcase Himself as the Desire of the Nations.[14]

14 Haggai 2

The new things He is about to do really will far exceed even the great things He has done throughout history.

Religion is of value to the degree that it leads us to the correct reputation of God. It's tragic for someone to pursue religion, thinking that they are pursuing God. How do you know if your perspective of Him is correct? He is God, and He is big enough to know how to open your eyes if you have a genuine desire for relationship with Him. One day Jesus explained to those He was teaching that good fathers would never give their children a serpent if they asked for a fish to eat, or a scorpion if they asked for an egg. He said how much more would our Heavenly Papa be happy to give us the Holy Spirit, if we ask. The Holy Spirit is also called the Spirit of Truth and frees us from false religion. When we seek the truth, we will find it, simply because it's the heart of our good Papa to give it to us. He said that when we knock and keep on knocking, the door will be opened to us.[15]

*When we really trust who God is, we stop trying to do what only He can do. We can't save ourselves by our efforts, nor can we be the one to convince someone else of truth. In the end, He does it. People need to hear the truth from others, but they will never recognize it if they don't really want it and if we are improperly representing the heart of God by coming across like we are forcing it on them. Freedom to choose our religion, or even no religion, is of utmost importance and must be protected at all cost, but the hopeful future of the religions of the world depends on us growing up about a couple of specific things: God is love, and love honors Him as well as others. God wants true relationship with us enough to not force Himself on us; therefore we shouldn't force others either. But we sure better have enough sense for ourselves to respond to His invitation. We also must remember that true religion is love in action — **God's** love in action on our behalf, and then our response to His love by **our** love in action on behalf of others. We must give what we have received. When we fully realize that God is the One who leads us into the standard of truth, we are then free to spend our energy being an expression of His love in action.*

15 Luke 11

Depending on the experiences you have had with churches and pastors, as ones who have been pastors ourselves we would like to sincerely repent for the ways any who have called themselves Christians have caused you pain. When that happens, it's usually because of the unhealed wounds of hearts that have settled for religion instead of a relationship with a God who loves. We believe that as each generation grows in the knowledge of who God really is, those who are followers of Jesus Christ will better represent God, even in the context of church. Christians are definitely still trying to figure out what God as love looks like in the church. We are sorry for our sometimes awful attempts to show you the God we have come to know. Because we are collectively made in His image, and because He is this multifaceted Rainbow God, we need each other to produce a truly healthy church expression. We will not be able to adequately produce churches that represent Him well until they are influenced from the inside out, multi-generationally, multi-racially, and by both male and female. But the days are coming when more and more churches will emerge that look and feel more like this God we are all desperate for. Join the ranks of those who gather in His name, determined to fill His house with the love of our Papa and His redeemed ones.

The hopeful future for religion is the Church that God refers to as the one not made by human hands—the one that even the gates of Hell cannot prevail against. We will grow into a people who so know the God of love that we too will be known for our love. The real God is irresistible when His love is poured out through us, rather than our attempt to get others to change their behavior. Christians have not always been known for their love, but in time, we will be.

INVITE HIM IN—AS REDEEMER

As a reminder, at the end of each chapter we will look at the next line of "The Lord's Prayer" in the context of focusing on a different aspect or face of God. In the first line Jesus taught us how to speak to God who is our Father in heaven, reminding us that we have access to the perfect Papa who heals our wounds of rejection and made us part of a spiritual family. In the second line Jesus went on to say, **"Hallowed be Your name."** *To hallow basically means to set apart as holy or treat with respect. It's another way to express honor. A person's name represents all that comes to your mind when you hear that person's name. What comes to mind when we hear God's name is whoever we personally know Him to be. If we know Him as He really is, then to us His name is holy and to be honored, never spoken of lightly or disrespected. If we easily use His name like any other curse word, it is a symptom of the distance we have from knowing the real Him.*

Long before God sent His Son Jesus to earth, He told Moses that one of His commandments was that we were not to take His name in vain. We were not to speak the name of God in a common way nor with flippancy like we so easily do now. God has always made a big deal about His name. Again, remembering that whatever He asks of us is in our best interest, why would He care that we not use His name lightly or as profanity? Whatever we behold or look at, that's what we become like. If the God we interact with is not a big enough deal to show sincere reverence to, then what's the point of giving ourselves to Him? If I can create Him and make Him like I want Him, then is He real to begin with? There's mystery concerning God, but He's mysteriously good. If I could get my mind fully around Him, then would He be God? And if He's God, then let's give Him the honor He and His name deserve.

Recent generations haven't given as much thought to the meaning of a person's name as previous generations did. We've typically named our children based on a tradition or simply liking the sound of it. We are also quick to choose names that are popular. Evidently Jesus was quite an ordinary name for His generation as well. This was obviously God's way of reiterating how ordinary and common He was willing to make Himself among mankind so we would appreciate how much the Creator of the universe was willing to humble Himself to be with us. Perhaps you have prayed or heard others pray in the name of Jesus. When we do that, we are acknowledging that it is through the redemptive sacrifice that Jesus made on the cross that we are able to relate directly to God ourselves. If Jesus is a name that con-

jures up anything less than a genuine sense of gratefulness for His sacrifice and friendship with us as sinners, then it's going to feel odd to hallow His name. But if you have come to know Jesus, remember for your own heart's sake to honor or hallow the name of the One who got you out of your prison—your Redeemer.

CHAPTER FIVE

KING: The Color of Power
THE SOLUTION FOR OUR GOVERNMENTS

I (Elizabeth) love The Chronicles of Narnia *by C.S. Lewis, written in the early 1950s. It's a series of novels about several children who are quite ordinary in their world but discover they are actually royalty in the Land of Narnia, where Aslan the Lion reigns as King. One moment the kids are fighting as siblings, the next they find themselves stumbling into a world that is more real than the one they came from. To their surprise, in Narnia they play a very important role in ruling as princes and princesses under Aslan's authority.*

One of the movies based on the books has a soundtrack with lyrics that seem to sum it all up. "I am a princess on the way to my throne, destined to reign, destined to roam." [1] *It captures the heart of the characters who are stuck in two realities—they are on their way to the place and time when they will one day rule, but meanwhile must continue to learn to function between the two contrasting worlds that seem to collide when they least expect it.*

I think the reason that this story has been so popular throughout several generations is because there is something in the core of all of us that knows we

---

1   "Wunderkind" by Alanis Morissette

exist for so much more than this visible reality. We intuitively know that we matter and have significance, even if the culture around us tells us otherwise. The truth is, when God created the earth, He gave us dominion over it. He left us, male and female, in charge under His sovereign authority.[2] We have been wired with the capacity for ruling over something, and we suffer from feelings of insecurity and lack of destiny when we are not given that opportunity. Perhaps that is why we all instinctively struggle for independence and the right to exercise a healthy level of authority over our own sphere of influence.

Government is meant to protect our God-given assignment to have dominion and rule—our personal right to rule. Government is not meant to rule over us but to give us the environment in which we can each rule our own domain. It must exist to acknowledge that God is King over kings, the Leader of leaders, the Ruler over rulers, and Owner of owners.

When a government is healthy and safe, it doesn't dominate people but rather protects their right to have their own dominion over the work of their own hands and ultimately over darkness that steals freedom from people. Good government provides a protective boundary around our ability to choose and live with the consequences of our choices. It protects our right to fail in order to give us the possibility to succeed and creates safety nets so that when we fall, we can have another chance to better rule our personal domain.

LOVE DISPLAYED AS POWER

We have been exploring the seven colors of love and what love specifically looks like in each area of culture, expressed through the different aspects of the heart of God. Healthy **family** gives us the **strength** of love we need to launch into the world, free from the rejection that prevents us from thriving. True **religion** provides us with the **honor** of love needed to maintain an intimate relationship with God through Jesus our Redeemer. **Government** that is free from corruption releases us to experience the **power** of love that uses authority for our good. **So in government, love looks like incorrupt power.** Any

---

2 Genesis 1:26-28

authority that exists other than for the good of the ones it serves is corrupt. Through government, the seat of authority and power of a nation, we were meant to grow up feeling safe and secure enough to be given the opportunity to be who we want to be. Government and all healthy authority protect the possibility of who we can become.

*Because **purple** or violet are the colors that have historically been used to represent government, we have chosen this color of the rainbow to refer to God as King. Throughout the centuries, when purple first became associated with royalty, only the wealthy leaders could afford the rare purple dye used for their clothing. The royal color purple is seen where red and blue collide on the color palette. We have already looked at how blue speaks of God as our Redeemer, the color of honor and heart felt awe of who He is. Red is the color of media or communication. Combining the two, we see that government serves as the good news or communication of God's ability to redeem everything that we go through so that we can be who He created us to be. When done well, government whispers to our hearts that we have the opportunity to succeed.*

Of course in the days of kings and kingdoms, communication was slow. Citizens of a kingdom may not have ever personally seen the king or even a portrait of him. They may have never had the opportunity to hear him speak, but they grew up in His kingdom knowing if he was a good king or not, based on the overall environment around them. If they were well protected and were given fair opportunities to prosper and a healthy system of laws and justice, they knew they had a good king. The overall climate of the kingdom was proof to the hearts of the citizens that they indeed had a good king.

Healthy government conditions the collective heart of a nation to believe that they can thrive and not simply survive. It does so in the same way that a healthy authority in an individual household conditions the hearts of the children in that family to believe that they can grow instead of just survive. When the government or authority structure in a family is abusive it causes the children to get stuck in survival mode emotionally. It's no different in a nation's government. When the ruling authority is abusive and corrupt, the citizens, sometimes generation after generation, get stuck in a cycle of just trying to survive rather than breaking through into true pros-

perity and destiny. In the same way that each of us exists to fulfill a unique destiny, so too each nation exists to contribute its own special sound and resources to the earth. When government functions the way it is supposed to, love is displayed as power—the power to prosper in every way. Government must exist to create the ability or power for its people to thrive. When it does, it conditions the hearts of those people to believe that God the King is indeed good.

THE LIE:
GOD DOES NOT CARE ABOUT US

How does bad government cause a person to believe that God doesn't care about them? Government, like the other areas of culture, presents a face of God to us that, when it is inaccurate, gives us a wrong perspective of God's heart and causes us to believe a lie about Him.

When a child grows up in a home under authority that hasn't protected him and given him plenty of opportunities to succeed, then his heart feels unstable and not cared for. Conversely, when children grow up in a home where they feel stable, protected, and cared for, they are more likely to believe that God cares about them. We are all prone to believe that God does care about us when things feel stable and that He doesn't care about us when things go wrong.

In the same way, the collective heart and soul of a nation feels safe and cared for when the ruling authority creates a protected environment that is full of opportunities for its citizens to flourish. Usually our first experience with authority in our home life didn't go so well and is followed up by another deep disappointment in the authority that leads our nation. It leaves us to believe that ultimately all authority is bad and has less than good intentions towards us. When a nation's government is riddled with scandals and thievery and obviously exists for the benefit of those in power rather than for the ones it serves, the effect on that nation is fear, apathy, and hopelessness because the people see no possibility for prosperity, growth, and change.

Most governments are done our way and are therefore full of corruption and abusive authority. Our way is founded on the belief that God, if He exists at all, has left us to figure out how to govern. When we govern with that foundational belief, we fall to corruption and rule with selfishness and pride instead of humility and service. Because of that, the collective heart of most nations are conditioned to believe the lie that God doesn't care about us, which then further perpetuates our unhealthy style of governing.

When children grow up knowing they are protected and cared for, there is no end to what they can do and be in life. Just imagine what citizens of a nation who believe that God truly cares about them can accomplish. The possibilities are endless and, as amazing as the United States is, no country has seen the full extent of what can be achieved when authority governs the King's way.

HOW DOES THIS LIE ABOUT GOD PLAY OUT IN CULTURE?

So if we collectively believe that God doesn't care about us, of course we will simply continue to do things the best way we can and not look to Him for help. And as we've established, God desires intimacy with us and therefore gives us the freedom to choose whether or not to look to Him for what we need. He guards our choice to ask for His help so that when we do look to Him, it comes from a sincere heart and desire for Him and His better ways. His desire for real relationship with us is greater than the risk He takes of us believing awful lies about Him like this one. We reap the consequences of this core belief that God does not care about us in our systems of government.

Of all societal structures, government most seems to remain in crisis. If we view things in the context of looking at all the nations of the world, we find that major crisis are happening in governments all the time. In my travels around the world, government corruption is a consistent complaint in every nation. This institution above all others seems to have the most difficulty in lifting itself out of the pit of unethical backroom deals, bribes, influence peddling, mishandling of funds, and over-reaching with its power.

We typically think the problem with government is too much power in the wrong hands — the idea that "power corrupts and absolute power corrupts absolutely." [3] *The healthiest governments we have created work as well as they do because we put into place ways to guard against any one person or political party having too much power for too long. We understandably are reluctant to trust authority, and there are few that are qualified to lead who should be trusted.*

The men and women who are charismatic enough to win elections seem to have the least-deserving character for a place in government. Their gift of persuasion connects a little too well with their gift of bending the laws and peddling illegitimate influence. In their minds, the ends justify the means. It's common for a president to arise with an initiative of cracking down on corruption only to be brought down under corruption charges himself.

Then we have those who are doing such a good job attacking corruption, terrorism, or violence that they begin to tinker with their nation's constitution while in office in order to consolidate power indefinitely. Even the champions of righteousness are bending or breaking the law so that they can remain in power. Power becomes a drug for those who have tasted of it.

What are we to do here on earth where people are so broken, wounded, and prone to sin? It's no wonder that entire Christian denominations forbid their people from being involved in politics. They are in effect saying that this area of culture is too dark for light to penetrate. Common sense will tell us this isn't true, as darkness cannot prevail over light. Our challenge seems to be in generating the light that could then displace the darkness.

If darkness is dishonest, crooked, immoral, and motivated by selfish gain, then light is servant-hearted, honest, law-abiding, moral, humble men and

---

3   quote from Lord John Acton 1834-1902

women who understand the purpose of government and have the personal fortitude it takes to walk in it. It is almost impossible these days to find a person who has the ability and understanding to lead along with the humility and integrity it takes to lead well. Even then, would they be dynamic enough for us to recognize them?

Until light shows up, darkness will continue to reign and be held back from completely overtaking any given nation only by the careful construction of laws that limit power. That seems to be the best we presently have to offer.

THERE IS ONE ENEMY IN THE WAR OVER GOVERNMENT

Civil wars and chaos have often centered around the nations' quests for a form of government that people want to live under. Essentially every political party and every form of government has at some point been someone's enemy in the war over government. No system or party is perfect because there are no perfect people. The real enemy remains the same as in every area of culture—Satan himself, ruler of the darkness and father of lies.

Behind the visible realm of things, a tremendous war is taking place over the governments of the world. Lucifer has understood the all-encompassing power that governments are capable of, so he has assigned himself to embark on the destruction of nations through them. In every sphere he has the same objectives. Use the structure itself to steal, kill, and destroy, marring that aspect of who God is in our eyes. Why is this his all-encompassing mission in life? Because, as we continue to say, it's his way at getting back at God. His profound bitterness at not being allowed to be the object of worship has left him with a mission to give God a black eye. His way of giving God a black eye is by taking that which is meant to be a blessing for God's children and turning it into a curse. He takes that which is meant to be a way for us to experience the goodness of God and uses it to cause us to believe that God doesn't care about us. Satan does that with sex, finances, arts, music, food, children, and more. He distorts every good thing and counterfeits it as his way of attacking the heart and correct reputation of our good Father.

Satan has no direct power to compete against God. If they boxed, God would knock him into the next galaxy with his first punch. Satan's actual power is not even measurable, as opposed to God's power. Because of this reality, Satan's only option is to continue to target the object of God's affection, rather than God Himself. His way of hurting God is by hurting His children. He has strategically decided that one of the best ways to hurt God's children is to control governments. He has done such a good job at this that studies show the number one cause of deaths among the nations is governments killing their own people. They have killed them in civil wars, in fighting terrorism, in suppressing antigovernment forces, and in other creatively worded and seemingly excusable ways. Sadly, sometimes the "terrorists" are in reality the ones who have the solutions for the problems that exist. In Africa, most of the problem of starvation can be attributed to corrupt forces in government that will not allow food and resources to get to certain tribes and regions. Satan consistently targets systems and structures because through systems and structures he can exponentially increase the body count of those God loves.

Satan has had temporary victory in distorting God's image that many ascribe to God as evil and bad motives. He, being the perfect Papa and the kindest King, is being wrongfully perceived because of Satan's significant ability to deceive. Satan has achieved his greatest victory in using what should be trustworthy leaders to perpetuate the lie that God doesn't care about us. We continue to settle for governments that are so filled with corruption that they cause their citizens to believe the real King of their "kingdom" could care less about them.

THE TRUTH:
GOD DOES CARE ABOUT US

When corruption abounds in the government of a nation, the citizens end up being enslaved to poverty because the leaders don't allow the money and resources to go where they are most needed. The pride and manipulation of those in authority serve their own agenda and do not have the good of the people as their motivation. They may talk as if they care for the poor, but the proof will be in the overall prosperity of the people in the context of each area of culture—family, religion, media, education, economy, and arts/entertainment. The collective heart and soul of nations bound by their government's corruption feel as if they are behind the rest of the world, tired of hoping for change, and ultimately abandoned by God Himself. Apathy and misery settle in on generation after generation, and soon the people can't remember ever feeling cared for by the leaders they look to or loved by God. You can know that you suffer because of the choices of evil men, but at the core of every hurting heart is the haunting question of why God does not intervene. We reason that if God is God and He is good, then He should be powerful and good enough to make the evil stop. He should be able to stop the corruption that keeps us back and holds us down.

God deals with the hearts of nations as He does with our hearts individually. He is not content to simply deliver us from sin but also wants us to really live and be free in every area of our hearts and lives. Similarly, God is not content to simply deliver our nations from corruption, but He also wants to deliver them from anything that keeps us from knowing the real Him. He wants the citizens of nations free from the effects of corruption so they can know Him and His heart for them—so that they can know that He cares. He understands that when we thrive under healthy government, we are more likely to believe that He cares about us.

Imagine what a shame it would be if a man is wrongfully put in prison and, when he finally gets out, he is so full of bitterness about it that he is still imprisoned in his heart—free on the outside but not on the inside. In the same way, God wants to free people from the corruption that has held their nation back. But He also wants the people free from the inside out—hearts that are convinced that God does care about them. God desires not only that every nation be free from corruption, but also free to truly flourish. Nations that are impoverished because of corruption—what we often refer to as third-world nations—feel overlooked by the world and abandoned by God. Like each of us individually, He knows what it will take for us to grow in the knowledge and understanding of who He really is and how good He is. So, too, the collective soul of a nation has a destiny to know God and His better ways of doing everything.

Only God knows exactly what it will take for each nation to grow in the knowledge of Him and, like with His firstborn Israel,[4] He will not intervene in the affairs of men, even when evil abounds and the ones He loves are suffering, if He is using it for the ultimate good of that nation. It all comes back to trust. Our hearts and our nations must learn to trust God if we are to have real relationship with Him. Without trust, there's no possibility for the thing we crave the most—intimacy with God.

WHO IS GOD—AS KING?

It's hard to trust a God that allows suffering and pain. If He wants us to trust Him, then why allow innocent ones to suffer? Remember the answer to these questions rests in the hands of a King whose kingdom has not fully come but will. It already exists in Heaven—that realm that is more real than what we have here. We are receiving an unshakable kingdom,[5] meaning it can't ever fall to corruption. This King is never the source of corruption or evil and the suffering that comes from it. Although this King is compassionate, He is not moved by pain because, unlike us, He knows the temporary state of it as compared to the eternal state of intimacy that we are being prepared for with Him. He uses the very weapons Satan meant for our destruction to produce in us the opportunity to know Him in ways we wouldn't if we didn't need

4   Exodus 4:22
5   Hebrews 12:28

to. You can't know Him as Comforter when you haven't mourned. You can't know Him as Provider when you haven't experienced lack. You can't know Him as King when you are content with man's version of leadership.

This King is for us and never against us. Even when we reject Him, He pursues us until our last breath. He wants to teach us how to serve like He does so we establish government on earth that is true to His heart for us. He wants us to grow in the knowledge of how He serves so we can serve like He does and remove corruption and evil from those who are suffering under the lies of the enemy. He even wants to deliver those leaders who have become so deceived themselves that they are being used as pawns by Satan. Many are fighting against God and think they are fighting for Him. God is the King of kings, and we are kings under the King. We will learn to rule like He does so His kingdom, His better ways of doing everything, can be established in the earth.

Heaven runs as a perfect kingdom and not as a republic or democracy. Kingdom concepts are easier to grasp when you live in a kingdom. A case can be made that government has the power to institute, override, and rule over all other sectors of society—and that is true. Government is ultimately where power is officially consolidated. Especially in a kingdom context, all the power sits at the top. Here on earth, we've established alternative government structures designed to provide checks and balances for too much centralized power, but of course in Heaven there is no such concern.

The Bible says of God that "righteousness and justice are the foundations of His throne."[6] This means everything is done from the King's heart of pure integrity and pure fairness. You don't need checks and balances of power based on that kind of foundation. God the King doesn't have to try to be just, He is by His very nature. He doesn't have to continually remind Himself of Stephen Covey's 7 habits of effective people—He contains in His nature the perfected versions of whatever experts admire as good character. God is com-

6 Psalm 89:14

pletely perfect in governmental character, governmental strategy, and governmental execution. You would think that we humans might want to invite in such a wise and accomplished Ruler, but here again we find ourselves reverting to our orphan spirit that acts like we just have to figure out everything on our own.

To know the real God as King, we must continue to look at how Jesus lived. Jesus taught us that in order to be a true leader, we would need to be a great servant.[7] He modeled His authority as King by laying His life down. He taught us to obey our Father by being obedient Himself. Jesus showed us that someone with real authority is submitted to authority too.

The God of the universe came to earth through Jesus and embraced humility, all for the sake of restoring to us the possibility of intimacy with Himself. Just as Jesus lived under the authority of the Father while He lived here, He also wants us to experience living under authority that has our best interest always in mind so we too could learn to lead with servant hearts that prioritize the best for those we're leading. We too will be kings when we live as those who have laid down their own rights for Him and for one another. When we learn to lead like God the King, His kingdom will be among us in its fullness.

A kingdom is the domain or sphere of authority of a king. It is essentially that king's ways of ruling or doing things — his system of governing. This King's ways are always better than our ways because He sees and knows what we cannot see and know. His plans for us are always better motivated than ours. Seeing God as King in our nations begins with encountering Him as King in our own hearts and lives individually.

HOW CAN WE COOPERATE WITH GOD AS KING IN RESTORING POWER TO GOVERNMENT?

When we speak of restoring power to government, remember that we're talking about God's power, the power of love. Love must be restored to

---

7   Mark 10:42-45

government, and more importantly to the hearts of those who govern. We can't give away what we don't have. It's difficult to display an authority motivated by love when we haven't submitted to an authority over us that is motivated by love. When we come under the power of love, we will lead with the power of love.

*Many people are afraid of Christians because they believe we're going to try to force people into our way of relating to God. History unfortunately has fueled this fear by events such as the Crusades and the various Inquisitions. Certainly many of those who committed atrocities in the name of God weren't genuine Christians; that was their cultural background, not their actual faith. But some were actual believers who were seriously misguided. Just like any other corrupt leaders, Christian leaders, whether in church or in any different areas of society, forget that **we are meant to have authority over the darkness that steals freedom from people but not over the people themselves.** There's a fine line between the two. The King we serve is protective over our right to choose Him and His kingdom because when we choose, He wants it to be sincere and not forced. He dominates over the things that keep us from choosing Him, willingly restraining His power to dominate over us. Anyone who does not rule in the same way is ruling in a form of corruption. We aren't created to dominate or rule over people but over Satan and principalities. Ruling, in its truest sense, is serving.*

Going back to the story of David and Goliath, the lies about who God is and those systems that perpetuate the lies are the giants of our day. Even before David was king of Israel, he would not tolerate the giant that taunted them and held them back as a nation from entering into their promised land.[8] So too we can be used by God when we have a healthy anger and intolerance for not only the corruption of our day but also for the lies about God that stem from those governments that are fortresses for corrupt leaders.

If you excessively study the giants of a promised land, you'll lose heart more than you'll benefit from your study. The problem of the promised land of government is not the presence of giants. The

8   1 Samuel 17

problem is the absence of co-laborers with God. It's a universal truth that darkness can't ultimately triumph over light. In quantum physics terms, it's impossible for photons to be held at bay by that which carries the absence of photons. Darkness has an energy level, but it is profoundly inferior to the energy level of light.

Our first step to advance in this area of culture must be in taking a new look at the rainbow. As we see the completeness of who God is, we begin to see His correct image. We will only reflect or re-image what we have first seen. This is where our wake-up call comes in. This is what Satan has been dreading for centuries. He knows if we see God's full image and reflect it all, then he is done for and his lies are over.

Satan's strategy has consisted of damage control. If he could convince most of us that God only has an eternal plan for us, then we only see God the Redeemer, and his only losses are to that image of God. But once God's sons and daughters begin to see His whole image in all of life, then it's just a matter of time before the image-bearers crush the darkness and lift the power of the lies about God off of the world. Whatever aspect of God we reflect is in fact light. Whatever color of His image we reflect makes the darkness' flight location-specific. Before we strategize government maneuvers, we want to first soak in the all-sufficiency of who God is.

Second, we want to raise up leaders with an opposite spirit to the way Lucifer operates. Satan distorts God's image. Those who know God will restore God's image by showcasing the real Him through the power of love. Our mission ultimately restores the good reputation of our Papa. Lucifer's basic tool of governmental destruction is corruption. He is able to do that with people who are connected only to ideals. Connecting to ideals alone won't hold anyone in the intense and treacherous battlefield of politics. Most politicians start out with ideals, but compromise comes easily to those whose values are separated from the God behind the values. This is further evidence of that orphan spirit we're prone to have. Government must be filled with sons and daughters of the King who have broken free from an orphan mentality and who see themselves as co-laborers with this King of kings.

THE HOPEFUL FUTURE FOR GOVERNMENT

Our present governmental landscape is filled with de facto orphans who idealistically push for good but do so assuming they are alone and unsupported. All of this will dramatically change in the coming years as a wave of true sons and daughters discover this promise land and invade with the light that comes from the heart of God. They will be those radicals who live not for themselves but for the King and the restoration of His good name. They will be on this mountain not for personal gain but as those who seek first the kingdom of God.[9]

This wave of God's sons and daughters will fill every level of governmental opportunity. They will be the candidates, the advisers, the funders, the intercessors, the chauffeurs, the cooks, the cleaners, the support systems at every level. This army of God's image—of God's violet or purple color—will displace systemic darkness. They will be responsible for new legislations, new righteous ordinances, even new constitutions. Wherever they see a distortion of God's image of government, they will go about restoring His image and the power of His love.

Those who serve in government will need to team up and work together because the wisdom of mountain climbing is to be roped together. Lone Rangers don't last long. Even great warriors, if too far ahead of the pack, get picked off by the enemy of God. This is a job for an army of God-lovers. Nothing will hold them back. They will counter every setback with a new resolve. They will be okay with two steps forward and one step back. They will relentlessly advance be-

9 Matthew 6:33

cause their cause is just and their cause is the fame of Him who rules in the affairs of man. When one falls, the others will pick him up, dust him off, and place him back in battle array. They will expect resistance from the enemy of God and will therefore be impossible to discourage. They will daily feed on the knowledge of this God of all life who is higher than, bigger than, and better than any lie that has ever been told about Him. They will assume every momentary setback is just the development of a future platform. They will walk and not faint. They will run and not be weary.[10] Wherever they go, life will spring up behind them. This will be an army like no others—lovers of God with a mission to expand His love in all the nations of the earth.

INVITE HIM IN—AS KING

If most of us had written the ideal prayer like Jesus did, certainly one of the first things we would have done is beg for God's help with something we're worried about. But not Jesus. Before He began His model prayer to help us learn how to talk to our Father, He took the time to explain that we didn't need to list the things we needed from God because He already knows what we need even before we ask Him.[11] Children of a good Papa don't have to ask for the love He freely gives nor for the things they need. Instead, Jesus said to pray, "Your kingdom come." So in this third line of "The Lord's Prayer" Jesus is showing us that what we are to ask is for His kingdom to come. His kingdom, or His way of doing things, is what we need more than anything else we think we need to ask for.

When we invite God into our hearts, lives, and circumstances as King, we are asking for Him to do things His way. When you trust Him more than yourself, you want to submit yourself to His plans, knowing He will always position you for something good in the end. When you ask for His kingdom, you are asking for His oversight in all that concerns you. The

10 Isaiah 40:31
11 Matthew 6:8

freedom of letting go of the power to govern your own life is tangible peace. Trust brings His government and His government brings peace.[12]

Hundreds of years before the birth of Christ, it was prophesied that He would be the Prince of Peace and that there would be no end to the increase of His government and peace.[13] *If you invite Him in as King to govern your world and teach you how to govern like Him, you will find increase and a prosperity of soul that can never be taken from you. A peace that supersedes your ability to understand will be like a guard to your heart and mind in the midst of the storms of life.*[14] *Invite God as **King** to establish His kingdom in your life, family, and nation until you see the **power** of His **love** bring peace on earth and goodwill to all men—until we see His kingdom come.*[15]

---

12 Isaiah 26:3
13 Isaiah 9:6-7
14 John 14:27 and Philippians 4:7
15 Luke 2:14

CHAPTER SIX

COMMUNICATOR: The Color of Blessing
THE SOLUTION FOR OUR MEDIA

The rate at which communication has changed and increased in our generation is mind-boggling. It took radio 38 years and TV 13 years to reach an audience of 50 million. Facebook users topped 100 million in less than nine months. Since its launch in 2004, this pioneer in social networking sites has more than 900 million active users, and more than half of them are using mobile devices.[1] I (Elizabeth) remember hearing when I was little that one day we would be able to talk to each other on small phones we carried in our pockets. At the time, I simply hoped they would make a longer telephone cord that would reach my bedroom and not get so tangled. The thought of a phone you didn't have to plug in seemed impossible and more of a fantasy, like the spider webs that shoot out of Spiderman's arms. The world's technology, understanding, and knowledge are not only increasing, they are doing so at a rate that's difficult to keep up with.

Over the last century, typical news media have dramatically shifted from making information primarily accessible through newspapers, radio, and TV to digital transmission through satellites and computers. Now that computers and cell phones are so easy to use, the possibilities for news and informa-

---

1   United Nations Cyberschoolbus Document and Wikipedia

tion to be shared seem instant and endless through options like Facebook, Twitter, Wikipedia, YouTube, email, and personal blogs, not to mention the millions of web sites that exist.

All communication started within the heart of a God who communicates. It shouldn't surprise us that communication is accelerating on earth because it is sourced from God Himself, who is alive and always pursuing intimacy with His sons and daughters. As we have said, intimacy requires trust, but it also requires speaking and listening, hearing and being heard, understanding and being understood. God created us so we could know Him and be known by Him.

*It's been asked, "If a tree falls in a forest and no one is around to hear it, does it make a sound?"[2] We may never know the answer to that question, but we do know that technically it would not have communicated anything! Communication hasn't truly happened unless information is given **and** received. God the Communicator is not okay with loving us without our knowing it. His desire is that we would actually receive, acknowledge, and know His love for us.*

Our first account of communication is in the Bible's description of God's creation of the earth as we know it. When time began, God's voice already existed—He was present, and what He had to say set time and life into motion on our planet.[3] Clearly when God speaks, whatever exists responds to His voice, and communication happens. By His words, everything was created[4] and, from then on, all living things carried within them the ability to communicate as well. Plants, animals, and humans who were made in His image interact and respond to one another and to their Creator.

A being powerful enough to create time and life is surely powerful enough to also know how everything was going to progress throughout history—from the choices made in the Garden of Eden, through every war between peoples and nations, through every natural disaster, to how it will all one day

2 Philosopher George Berkeley, in his work, *A Treatise Concerning the Principles of Human Knowledge* (1710)

3 John 1:1

4 Genesis 1

end up. Nothing took God by surprise, nor will it in the future. So why did He start all of this? Why did He put something into motion that would cause us such pain, disease, and bloodshed?

Communication, like all other aspects of who God is, cannot be separated from the essence of who He is—love. Love saw the end before time began, and evidently the end makes the ups and downs of history worth it all—there simply must be a very happy ending to what He started. A good God will make sure of it. Can you imagine the Creator who looked at each part of His creation and said, "It is good!" being a God who allows His creation to just fizzle out? Would He leave us, the object of His affection, to think He had a lousy plan? Not this God. Not a God who is good and wants us to know His goodness—a Papa who wants His children to know His heart for them. Ultimately, communication that has any value happens in the context of God's master plan—a plan that definitely has a happy ending that was intentionally designed, from beginning to end, out of His great love for us. So what does God as love look like displayed in communication, specifically in media?

LOVE DISPLAYED AS LOVE

The color of love that we associate with **media** is **red**. Red typically makes us think of fire and blood—danger, passion, and love. Red is used as the color for making us pay special attention. Our STOP signs and YIELD signs are red. Our red lights signal traffic to stop. Many Bibles have a red-letter edition, highlighting all the words of Jesus in red. It's the color used to draw attention to inspiring or important news. When we watch the news, special newsflashes will generally be presented in red. A severe weather or terrorism threat is signaled as a "code red" alert. In multiple ways and forms, red is a color that commands our attention and expresses an exaggerated form of communication. And what woman wouldn't "hear" love being communicated when presented with a dozen deep red roses?

In the area of culture we refer to as Media, love looks like blessing. When love is communicated, it registers on the heart of the recipient as blessing. The dictionary describes a blessing as "a beneficial thing for which one is grateful" and also as "God's favor."[5] When love is expressed and hits its target in our hearts, it's a benefit to us, and we're grateful for it. Our hearts are wired to accept any love as ultimately the favor of God toward us. When we go through hard times and feel unloved or cursed (the opposite of blessed), we tend to believe that God doesn't love, favor, or bless us. Even if we think we have our belief (or lack of belief) in God all neat and tidy in one corner of our heart, the reality is that we all have an innate sense that we are loved or not loved by God based on whether or not we have determined if He has blessed us.

Why does God's blessing mean so much to us? A blessing goes beyond what someone thinks about us and into what they actually say about us or to us. Words are literally a source of life and death to us because it was the voice and words of our Creator that spoke us into reality and even now sustain us. Words, as well as other forms of communication, cause us to feel loved or rejected. A lack of words and other forms of communication can equally contribute to a sense of being rejected and unvalued. Sometimes what is never said is the most painful of all.

Our word for blessing comes from the Greek word "eulogia," from which we get the word eulogy. It literally means "good word." At a funeral, when we eulogize someone who has died, we share what we thought about that person and what they meant to us. No matter how awful the person may have been, we always find something positive or redemptive to speak about them. We find the silver lining or good news of their life story and try to create some level of a happy ending to it, right? In a similar way, when our communication is sourced from love, what we speak will be the truth presented from a perspective of an eventual happy ending and will therefore bless those who hear it. Even when it's information that is difficult to hear, it will bring life and remembrance of the goodness of God.

---

5 Apple online dictionary

Words are also a big part of our identity. What people say about us and to us is part of who we think we are. In biblical days, your name was who you were, so parents would name their children with that in mind. Often the children were named according to the circumstance of life that they happened to be born into, which could be good or bad. They also gave priority to fathers blessing each of their children before the father died. A father's declaration of identity and inheritance was passed down through words in the form of a blessing. That culture understood the impact of words and the importance of God's blessing and favor on their lives.

A great example of the importance of blessing is found in the historical account of Jacob. He was born a twin and, without going through the lengthy version, he and his brother didn't get along. Jacob had moved far away for many years and finally decided to go back home and face his brother. He desperately wanted to reunite but was terrified that he and all his family would be killed by his brother and his family as soon as he saw them returning. The night before Jacob was to arrive home, he wrestled with God. Although it may be hard to believe what the Bible tells us, that he physically wrestled all night with the angel of the Lord, we can all identify with facing a terrifying situation and wrestling within our hearts with God over it.

*Jacob told God that he would not let Him go until God blessed him.[6] We too cry out to God in frustration and desperation for His blessing when we're facing a potential crisis. Evidently Jacob's insistence on receiving words from God that would give him a new identity moved God's heart. Jacob knew that if God blessed him, it would assure him that everything was going to be all right. God responded to Jacob by giving him His blessing—the new name Israel and a new identity—all because he wrestled with **God** and with **man** and prevailed. Jacob wrestled with **man** in that he did not give up on relationship with his brother, even though it was painful and risky. He wrestled with **God** in that He was not satisfied with having received his identity from the life circumstances he was born into. The name Jacob means supplanter or one who usurps, and was connected to the circumstance of his birth. Jacob wanted*

---

6   Genesis 32:26

to know that his identity was not coincidence or happenstance but that he fit into a bigger, more intentional plan from the heart of God Himself. Like you and me, he wanted to know that God Himself had blessed him and had given him an identity that fit into an important future. And just like that, God took a man who wasn't sure he would survive the next day and made him the beginning of what became His firstborn nation, Israel—the start of God's relational investment not only in individuals but also in the collective hearts of nations.[7]

The best part of that story is that when Jacob received his new name and new identity, it immediately stirred in him the desire to know **God's** *name and identity. As soon as Jacob received his new name, he said, "Tell me* **Your** *name." Even though Jacob already knew it was God that he had been struggling with all night, it stirred in him a hunger to know God's real name—a deeper identity than what he already knew of Him. What that potentially means for us is this: as we find our true identity in words that connect to our hearts as a blessing, it causes us to hunger to know the real God. We want to be known apart from the circumstances of our lives in the same way that God wants to be known apart from the lies the enemy has told us about Him.*

So how does all of that connect to the idea of media in our culture? Just as words spoken over us affect our personal identity, they also affect the identity of a city or nation. Media can be a tool to receive the blessing of knowing that we fit into a good plan of a good God. Or media can be something that slowly wears down our ability to believe that any situation can have an important worthwhile purpose and an ending that points us to a good Papa who is intimately involved in our lives, even when it may not seem like it. Essentially, the source of the words don't matter because our hearts let them in as if they are from God, which means media can potentially be used to bless or curse the soul of a nation. The wise King Solomon said it this way: "Death and life are in the power of the tongue."[8]

---

7   Exodus 4:22 When God called Israel the firstborn among many nations, the implication is that there are many other nations that He considers like His children.
8   Proverbs 18:21

News, and therefore media, has the power to touch our core beliefs about God, even if nothing is directly said about God or religion. The way in which news is presented can cause our hearts to fear or to trust—fear the future as random victims of circumstance or trust that somehow the difficult things we go through are an important part of a bigger purpose.

THE LIE:
GOD DOESN'T HAVE A GOOD PLAN FOR US

In preparing to write my part of this chapter, I (Elizabeth) asked our 18-year-old daughter what lie she is tempted to believe about God when she watches the news or reads information on the Internet. Without thinking at all, she easily identified the lie that God does not have a good plan for us. She explained how watching and listening to the stream of bad news and tragic stories causes her to have to remind herself that God is in charge, no matter how chaotic things get, and that He is good even when it temporarily seems like He isn't. As she said it, I realized how accurate her perception is.

It's certainly not the media's fault that bad things happen, but in doing their job to make the facts available to the public and present them in an unbiased way, even what is called responsible reporting can propagate a lie about God. When information is presented as a matter of fact, apart from a compassionate and heartfelt response, we are left to assume that is God's heart—that He is distant and focused on the facts, untouched by what is happening all around Him, so to speak. With reporters unaware of it, they speak and our hearts translate their words as the curse of all curses—my God, if He exists, is all about the facts and, like a good journalist, He never gets involved so as not to taint the reality of the mess I have made or am the victim of.

Some of the most impacting and historical moments in journalism are of famous professional news anchormen who, when having to report on a national tragedy, were moved to a quivering voice or the hint of tears. Why were we so touched by those moments? Because they are so very rare, and our hearts inwardly long for the news of our world to connect to the heart of a

God who cares, is compassionate, and is manning the steering wheel of this journey through history.

This lie that God does not have a good plan for us is also perpetrated against Him in another way. As with all good things, there is always a downside. The downside to such easily accessible mass media is that we are exposed to much more negativity than a soul was meant to bear. For this reason, several years ago I decided to stop watching the news. I used to keep the news channel going almost all the time in our home until I realized how much it was stressing me out. I was so used to that feeling that I didn't even realize it until I noticed how my hands lightly trembled from too much adrenaline. Johnny explained it to me like this one day: God gives us access to all we need in Him to get through whatever we go through, if we want His help. That's called His grace, or His power, that enables us to do what is needed in any given circumstance of life. His grace is available when we need it for what we are personally going through. Grace isn't available for what we fear we may go through, nor for what we watch someone else go through. So when we constantly feed on a steady diet of hardships of others, we do so apart from the grace needed to get through it. It's not our crisis, therefore we don't have the grace for it. We watch in horror and at least subconsciously connect to it in such a way that it registers on our psyche and body as if we were the ones going through it. We encounter someone else's pain and translate our response as if it were our reality—a reality of tragedy without God's grace to get through it or see what He is doing in the midst of it.

Once I weaned myself from the onslaught of sad stories that I couldn't do anything directly about, I was able to focus on accessing a fresh perspective of the grace of God that is always with me for whatever I am going through or will go through in the future.[9] I am able to better understand and recognize how He was with me in the middle of my life storms and how He used them to show me the truth about who He is and how much He cares for me. The intimacy with Him that I have gained through the trials have made the storms worth it and allowed me to embrace pain as an opportunity to know

---

9   You may be happy to know that I can now be a responsible citizen and stay up to date on news, without feeling fearful or stressed by it!

the real God. Once you can see that for your own life, you're able to see that for others as well. When you learn to find His goodness in your own pain, you can easily find it in someone else's. We would not have been able to serve as pastors for 15 years if we hadn't begun to learn this. It's impossible to help others when you're either trying to rescue them from something God isn't rescuing them from or you're feeling just as hopeless as they are. You can give someone hope when you yourself know that everything is an opportunity to see an aspect of the goodness of God you haven't seen before. And His goodness is seen in the plan that He has for us.

THE TRUTH:
GOD HAS A GOOD PLAN FOR US

Maybe you're like me, and when people speak of the sovereignty of God, it's hard to wrap your mind around it. Sovereign means absolute. God has absolute final say in everything. Yes, we can most often attribute a crisis to the result of either our own bad choice or someone else's, but we are also instinctively aware that God could have intervened if He really wanted to. God is sovereign. Depending on how things are going for you and how much you trust God, that's either good or bad news to you. Also, depending on how much your heart goes out to others who live in extreme circumstances, you may wrestle with many of the questions we've brought up about why He allows the mess we see and experience. Whether we like it or not, we all know in our core that God is ultimately in charge and has a plan He is working out. Want me to prove it? No matter what race, gender, or economic status, we all get mad at Him when things go wrong. And we all cry out to some version of Him when we're desperate enough. We're wired from the core to know that He is sovereign. His very existence is written into our hearts.[10]

Perhaps we have all heard people say "God knows what's best for you." That used to really rub me the wrong way. It felt like they were implying that

---

10 Ecclesiastes 3:11 says that God has put eternity in our hearts. Therefore we know we exist for something more than this temporary life.

I should just choke down His horrible plan for me and my future like it was a nasty medicine that was somehow good for me. The reality is, our "good" is to know God as He really is. He's so much more than we have hoped He is. His heart for us is much more loving and caring towards us than we individually and collectively ache for. Our "good" is intimacy with Him that we were originally created to have—giving and receiving love from the Source of everything that is good and true.

When we finally believe God is good, we can live from a place of joy because we know that He's using everything in our life that we have been through or will go through to work together for our good.[11] We can face the future and whatever ups and downs it holds without fear, when our perspective of God is filtered through the belief that He is good. When we know He's good, the sad stories of life are experienced through the anticipation of growing in the knowledge of God and in intimacy with Him. If that sounds like less than exciting to you, then you simply haven't seen enough of Him yet. When we really see Him with the eyes of our heart, His love is irresistible, and it only makes us hungry to know Him more.

It's important at this point to clarify the definition of a "good plan." Does God have a good plan for those born with a death sentence from the beginning—like a child born with a birth defect or into an abusive family situation, or a person raised without enough food and clean water? Yes, He does. As we spoke of in the last chapter, God knows exactly what it will take for every individual and every nation to grow in the knowledge of who He really is—for His correct reputation to be restored to His creation. Unlike us, He easily sees every sad story and impossible situation as a possibility for us to expand our perception of Him. Does that mean He is the One behind all the tragedy, sickness, and disasters? No. Simple cause and effect of our choices provides enough for Him to work with. But He certainly doesn't intervene as often as we think we would if we were God. Again, it must mean He's aware of something that we aren't, something that makes it all worth it in the end.

---

11 Romans 8:28

The truth is, God does have a good plan for those who want it, and it's called the gospel of the Kingdom. Jesus, who came to redeem us and show us a glimpse of the heart of our Father, spent the last three years of His life healing people and preaching the gospel of the Kingdom.[12] The word "gospel" means "good news."[13] And remember, the Kingdom of God is essentially God's better way of doing everything. As God's Kingdom is established on earth, we will see His solutions for all problems come, and once and for all we'll know His heart of love for us. Sometimes Christians have only valued the good news of salvation or redemption through Jesus, but the good news is actually so much more than that. The gospel of the Kingdom is the good news that God's better ways of doing everything are available to us. *Jesus had crowds following Him not just because he was healing them but because He kept bringing them the good news about how the Kingdom functions in heaven and how it could likewise function on earth. Jesus is our proof that God has a good plan. Jesus Himself was a part of God's better way of doing everything. As we said in the chapter on religion, Jesus became our better way of relating to God through His sacrifice rather than through our hard work.*

The good plan and happy ending we're hoping for is nothing less than the Kingdom of God on earth and the knowledge of His glory filling the earth.[14] We can speculate what that will be like, but most certainly it's much better and different than any of us have ever imagined.[15] Is it utopia on earth? At some point, yes. No one, no matter how convincing they seem, will ever know the exact timing of these things. But we do know that all things will be restored[16]—from our Papa's correct reputation to creation living in the harmony He originally intended.

Christians sing about it, and we all feel it at times—the earth, as it is right now, doesn't feel like home. We instinctively know we were made for

---

12 Matthew 4:23 and 9:35, Mark 1:14
13 Apple's online dictionary
14 Habakuk 2:14 God's glory is what makes Him, Him. It is all that makes Him as awesome and amazing as He is.
15 1 Corinthians 2:9
16 Acts 3:21

so much more than this, but at the same time, it is home. And no matter how dysfunctional home can be, it's ours. Unfortunately, some well-meaning Christians have taken that sense and developed a theology that makes it somehow okay for us to give up on God's creation and wait to fly away one day with God. They are correct in this: this world, as we know it, will no longer exist in the future. Jesus will return to earth again, and there will be a new earth and new Heaven.[17] *That does not mean this planet will be eradicated, but rather it will no longer be the way it is now. There will be an extreme world makeover by our God, through His children who so thoroughly know who He is that they will access His better ways of doing everything. They will care about what He cares about, all people and all nations, and display God as love in every area of culture.*

The good news of the Kingdom is the fact that God is in charge. He has solutions for everything. He works all things together for our good, and our good is to know the real Him. His kingdom, Heaven coming to earth, is our happy ending. I've heard it said this way: "God is mysterious, but He is mysteriously good." In the same way, the fact that God is in charge and has a good plan feels somewhat mysterious to us. But no doubt, His plan is mysteriously good, and He is indeed in charge.

HOW DOES THIS LIE ABOUT GOD PLAY OUT IN CULTURE?

It is said that whoever controls the media controls the state or government. Throughout history, seemingly every government takeover has been coordinated with a foundational understanding that the flow of news must be controlled in order to lessen resistance. Today, perhaps as never before, the decentralization of news has allowed for many revolts to take place that previously would have been kept under wraps through the overt control of news agencies. With the advent of the web and social networks, it

---

17 Revelation 21:1

has become very difficult for governments to control the flow of information among its citizens. The free flow of news is causing both many new opportunities and also many new challenges— such as when terrorists or organized criminals coordinate attacks. The 2011 Arab revolutions were fomented and sustained almost exclusively by this new reality of the decentralization of news. Many new possibilities are made available to us because of what has recently taken place in this important sector of society. *We have also been negatively affected in some specific ways by the lie about God that He doesn't have a good plan.*

Let's go a step deeper—He who controls the media, also controls the collective heart of a city or nation, affecting the individuals' health and state of mind. The effect of bad news is universal—it disheartens and troubles.[18] Many medical studies, as well as the Bible, tell us that good news literally affects our bodies.[19] There's an intrinsic value to it. Good news can strengthen you physically, and good news is refreshing to a weary soul. Conversely, we can gather that bad news will sicken us and bad news will demoralize us. Being exposed continually to bad or tragic news will make people fearful, sick, and weak.

Think about that in your personal life. If someone tells you some bad news, it can literally make you weak in the knees and sick to your stomach. But if you can receive the same news spoken in the context of hope and a bigger plan, you will approach the new difficult reality with a strength you need to get through it. If doctors could learn that simple truth, I'm convinced we would all be healthier and live longer. A factual prognosis, when not spoken with hope, is like a death sentence. An accurate assessment of an illness or a difficult situation that is given with the potential for a happy ending, no matter how small the chances, is an invitation to live.[20]

---

18 Jeremiah 49:23
19 Proverbs 15:30, 25:25
20 What if all doctors who had to give bad news to a patient, made it a practice to also at the same time always tell the story of someone who overcame it? What would be wrong with that?!

Generally speaking, mass media have been so adamant about presenting straightforward facts in order to protect our rights to hear unbiased information that they err on the side of being like a doctor who has no compassion or personal connection to the patient he is caring for. Media also tend to be hypocritical in that they want to produce accurate content, but the degree and frequency with which they present it is based on ratings. Is it responsible reporting to replay something horrific and tragic just because it will increase the numbers of people watching? Is it responsible journalism to write and talk incessantly about things that might happen to a minuscule percentage of the population, just because our fear of the unknown provokes us to stop and listen? Especially when you consider the affect it has on our culture, why do it? It may be worth it to the guys at the top handling the accounting, but what about the rest of society?

*When our individual hearts already struggle with the fear that God may not actually be in charge or have a good plan for our life, then we play that lie out in what we communicate to each other. Mass media perpetuates that fear by drawing us into a cycle of bad news that creates more fear and belief in the lie. We each tend to see the glass half full or half empty. We see God as in charge, and therefore everything is going to be okay; or we see life as victims left to fend for ourselves, and therefore we're screwed. It's not media's fault which way we see it, but if media can be used to help us see the glass as half full, why not? Wouldn't the ratings eventually respond to our need to believe that we are not victims of chance and that however much is missing from the "glass," there is still something left? It's all in the way we see things. The kingdom of God is not only God's better way of **doing** everything but also His better way of **seeing** everything. We are not saying media outlets need to start preaching about God, but rather utilize freedom of speech for the purpose of helping free us from lies. Our freedom of speech, which all media are built on, has produced a society of people who are free on the outside but enslaved inside. Media reports are meant to defend our access to truth, but real truth sets you free from the inside out.*

When we believe, individually and collectively, that God doesn't have a good plan for us, we live enslaved to fear. Fear not only affects our health, it's emotionally exhausting. When we fear, we constantly scramble to control everything we can in order to minimize the possibility for more pain. That control usually gets us into relational problems that turn into more pain, causing more fear and control. We are all pretty typical in our responses to this cycle—addictions, excessive entertainment, shame, greed, or basically any diversion from pain or the fear it causes. As a self proclaimed expert, let me say that God is angry about that cycle—not angry with us, but angry because He hates seeing the ones He loves suffer from the lies we have believed about Him and ourselves. Those working in media who get that heart of His will discover His better ways of communicating news and information. Truly responsible reporting is essentially the finger that dares to reach into the spinning fan of fear and interrupt its perpetual cycle.

THERE IS ONE ENEMY IN THE WAR OVER MEDIA

It's imperative that we know Satan wars to control every structure of society and use it to perpetuate lies about God. If he can control the overall structures, he doesn't even need that many demons on the job because the philosophy that's in place does the bulk of the damage to us and our nations. Satan distorts the desired image of God in every sector of society, thus turning a potential blessing into a curse. There is a glory to media, but in general we aren't presently seeing it. That will change as God's children arise and shine with His correct image for that sector of society.

Satan has a fairly simple strategy in every area of culture. Just as God has different aspects to who He is, Satan does as well. The Bible calls them principalities.[21] Some people think of them as separate from him, but it really doesn't matter either way. In media, he uses a principality to release fear, despair, and filth over the airwaves. He kills, steals, and destroys using bad or distorted news as a prime instrument. Most media outlets are corrupted by the underpinnings

21 Ephesians 1:21, 6:12, Colossians 2:10,15, Romans 8:38

of their operating philosophy. They may or may not handle their contracts and books correctly, but the corruption comes in as they bow to interests other than that which should dominate. They know they are supposed to exist to bring unbiased, objective reporting, but they ultimately bow to special interests and the pursuit of ratings. Because most on this mountain don't understand the spiritual warfare dynamics, they become willful subjects of the grand distorter of all truth.

The philosophy of operation for the spiritual principality over media is to find the dirt, the gossip, the controversy, the blood, the sex, the terror—and then exploit them to the max. Satan rewards those who go that route with quick ratings that then encourage even more of the same. Soon this pattern is institutionalized in an organization that was formed on altruistic intentions, and what used to be a news outlet now becomes an outlet for gossip, smut, or fear. These may offer returns on the short order of ratings, but then someone will always come around who will lower the bar even more—and there go the ratings.

At times, news agencies and organizations do yield to God's ways, but this is the exception more than the rule. An example of "God's way" would be in the aftermath of the destructive earthquake in Haiti. It truly was and still remains an event that deserves the attention of news agencies, particularly if they would cooperate with the heart of God in their reporting. Some news agencies did a great job of presenting not only the facts of the destruction but also the stories of heroism that inspired us. There were stories of Israeli mobile hospitals that performed heroically, saving many lives. Funds were raised that assisted many. There were stories of Haitians helping each other and of spontaneous worship services to God. Many heartwarming stories came out during this time. The earthquake carried a treasure trove of available redemptive news reporting, and at least some of it made it into the mainstream of media.

What is not helpful with news of that scope and scale is to keep replaying the most terrifying moments over and over and over again. In doing so, one cooperates with Satan's love of releasing fear and despair at a mass scale. He loves the material he has to work with when natural disasters come, and he uses it to dishearten people all over the globe. He loved the destruction of the twin towers in New York on 9/11 because, though it only happened once, he was able to promote fear and his lies into our hearts as we were exposed countless times to the horrific scenes. This is why terrorism is called **terror**ism—and why it works. The reality of most news watching today is that if you're a frequent news watcher, you're also most likely a fearful person. One begets the other, and it's by design—the design of the enemy that works in this sector of society.

People who work in various news agencies and TV channels are not the enemy. Even the most irresponsible reporters and those in media who are driven by money and ratings are not the problem. They are simply participating with the father of lies without realizing it.

The bottom line is that Satan does not want us to live free from fear because, when we do, his lies are over. He convinces us through our own circumstances that there is no plan. He convinces us through mass media, as we watch others go through pain that we too fear, that God is not in charge. But the truth always wins. Truth is light. And darkness, no matter how dark, gives way to light.

WHO IS GOD—AS COMMUNICATOR?

Before Jesus showed up on earth, God sent His archangel Gabriel to communicate the good news of Jesus' birth. When he spoke of Jesus' imminent arrival, Gabriel announced himself as one who stood in the presence of God and was sent to bring good news of great joy.[22] Heaven's intervention into society has always been a matter of good

---

22 Luke 1:19, 2:10

news, and it always overrides whatever disaster is presently playing out on planet earth. God's communication always includes a plan of redemption for everything that is taking place in society. He desires to assist His representatives in media in finding the redemptive news of the day and of the times. Communication and news reporting have always existed and will always exist.

Everything sourced from God is done in the context of good news. Even when God requires repentance from us, it's always expressed in the context of great accompanying news if we repent. God is so connected to the idea of good news that with every good thing He's going to do, He first announces that He's going to do it and then He does it. He then tells us the good things that He did. The Bible is full of examples of how He would speak through dreams, visions, prophets, angels, and even audibly before and after He did things. Just because we haven't added to the Bible more recent accounts of His communication doesn't mean it isn't still happening. God is constantly communicating in all of those ways and more for those who have a heart to recognize it.[23]

God as Communicator is the aspect of Himself that speaks as one who already knows the happy ending. God as Communicator will always speak the whole truth to us motivated out of love for us. Would a good parent tell a child something negative with no option for advancing out of it? No, and neither would God. His words, how and what He communicates, are always full of life, hope, possibility, and the perspective that whatever we are going through can be overcome and can end with us growing in our understanding of Him. How do you know when it's God that's communicating with you? You know because God's communication leaves you feeling like there is something greater that you are being prepared for that makes all that you are going through worthwhile.

---

23 If you want to learn more about how to recognize when and how God speaks to us, you can go to our website, provided at the end of the book, and order the DVD series and workbook called "Hearing God."

HOW CAN WE COOPERATE WITH GOD
AS COMMUNICATOR
IN RESTORING BLESSING TO MEDIA?

We can cooperate with God as Communicator by, like Him, being those who bring good news—not only the good news of salvation but also of the Kingdom, which is God's better way of doing, seeing, and saying things. Those in media must carry a spirit of good news in their own life in order to bring it into their professional role. What they contend for personally will easily overflow from them in the workplace. Every stage of getting a story or information out to the public must be infused with a perspective of hope that helps the listener or viewer recognize the potential for a happy ending. Any nation's culture that shifts in this way will experience the blessing that media are meant to be.

It's not that the media need to promote religion, God, or salvation through Christ in a blatant way. Any news that promotes peace in our hearts registers to us as the good news that God reigns in the earth.[24] Ultimately the news that our God reigns is the best news because it means He's in charge and we haven't been left as victims of random tragedies with sad endings. He will anoint those who are willing to cooperate with Him to release good news to all of creation, and it will change the very climate of culture.[25]

So how do we form news agencies that reflect God as Communicator? The following will apply whether you're trying to create the agency or just find your place on this mountain of society. I believe Philippians 4:8 gives the best guidelines imaginable for reporting and, most importantly, these guidelines are reflective of God's heart—which is the ultimate goal. In order to reflect Him, we must first see Him. Before you can know your media assignment, you have to know Him personally as Communicator. Once you know Him as Communicator and what His goals are, then you

24 Isaiah 52:7
25 Isaiah 61:1, Mark 16:15

get the privilege and reward of seeing Him re-imaged in society. It is this re-imaging of God that displaces the darkness of that sector of society. God is all about giving, hearing, and broadcasting good news. He doesn't have to think about doing it, but does so out of His divine DNA. Good news and redemptive news are a foundation of His kingdom.

> Whatever things are TRUE, whatever things are NOBLE, whatever things are RIGHT, whatever things are PURE, whatever things are LOVELY, whatever things are of a GOOD REPORT, if there be anything ADMIRABLE, and if there be anything PRAISEWORTHY, think about (publish) these things. (parentheses added)

I believe that if anyone called into media adapts this as their core philosophy, they will immediately connect themselves to unusual help from God. There will be unusual resistance also, but the help will overcome the resistance. Obviously news reporting still has to be done in excellence and in a way that establishes credibility, but you partner with God as Communicator by aligning what and how you communicate with what and how He communicates.

THE HOPEFUL FUTURE FOR MEDIA

In the coming days, the news organizations that follow the above criteria will be the ones that eventually win the ratings wars. When you communicate as a partner with God, you don't think ratings first. But His ways are always the better ways anyway and are ultimately rewarded on earth as they are rewarded in Heaven. People are sick and tired of being sick and tired of the communication parading as news but in reality sickens the soul.

Because of all the recent changes brought on by Internet life and smart phones, there has obviously been a tremendous leveling of the playing field. Newspapers and media outlets are shutting down in droves as the control and spread of information decentralizes. Suddenly, there are multiple sources for perspective and truth. This gives sons and daughters of God options that other generations haven't had. You can create a news blog with excellence and suddenly find yourself carrying influence over the thoughts of thousands or even millions. Who would have ever dreamed it could be possible to have that kind of influence without leaving your house? Ultimately, anyone who has any following at all on Facebook or Twitter has positioned him- or herself with a platform to partner with God in seeing one of His true colors shine through. May many of you respond to that opportunity to bring God's redemptive perspective of life circumstances to others. It truly is a way to expand God's Kingdom, even if people aren't "getting saved."

INVITE HIM IN—AS COMMUNICATOR

"Your will be done, on earth as it is in heaven."[26] These were the impassioned words of Jesus in the fourth line as He prayed the fourth line of "The Lord's Prayer." Jesus was making a statement of functionality. He wasn't speaking about salvation because salvation doesn't take place in Heaven but rather here on earth. His discourse was along functional lines. He was in essence saying, "Father, we need the way things function in Heaven to come work the same way here on earth. We need the way government works in Heaven to come work on earth. We need the way arts and creativity work in Heaven to manifest here on earth. We need the keys of heavenly education to come down and function here on earth. We need the way provision takes place in Heaven to be a reality here on earth.

26 Matthew 6:10

We need the way family works in Heaven to come to earth. We need the way You are honored in Heaven to be a reality here on earth. We need the way news reporting works in Heaven to come and work here on earth." Furthermore, He wasn't just praying it as a request. He was declaring what would happen. The way the kingdom functions in Heaven will come on earth and function here also. He was God in the flesh and He cannot lie.

God's will is a given in Heaven. Seeing Him face to face as He really is in Heaven assures us that only His will is done there. Why would anyone there want their own will, when they can have His? That tells us a lot about just how amazing He must be. If His will is good enough for those in Heaven, how much more so for earth? Everyone will rejoice when all of Heaven one day invades all of earth because we have learned to invite Him in as Communicator.

Invite God as Communicator into your personal world as well. God loves to teach us how to see things from His perspective. He loves it when we learn how to recognize His ability and desire to redeem every situation for our good and restore everything the enemy steals. He also loves to teach us to communicate like He does, as ones who bless those around us with the good news that He is in charge and has a good plan.

Johnny and I love to watch shows where the good guys are pinned down without a chance of surviving and someone comes just in time to rescue them. I especially like it when it's a girl who saves the day! One of my favorite things about God is that to Him we are all equal, which means even the chicks get a sword! Watching shows that have a variety of creative ways to rescue people, I have realized the importance of our cooperating with God as the One who rescues us. Can you imagine if you were in captivity and a special forces team showed up to help you, how important it would be to know whether they were there to extract you or to give you what you need to fight your way out? We are being helped, but when we don't know whether it's in the form of a rescue or the ability to overcome, then we may not recognize God in the midst of our difficult story lines. When you invite God in as Communicator, you first begin to recognize that He is always right in the middle of whatever we or someone else is going through. He is always accessible. Then we must learn to discern if He is offering to get us or that person out, or to strengthen us or them to get through it. When we can see what He's doing, then we can align ourselves with it and not exhaust ourselves in fear and control. Invite Him to communicate with you about how to see what He is doing from a hopeful perspective, and then communicate it to others. What you can see, you can give away.

CHAPTER SEVEN

TEACHER: The Color of Wisdom
THE SOLUTION FOR OUR EDUCATION SYSTEMS

Depending on how old you are and how much education you've received, you may have easily spent more than half your life in a school setting. How much of your education do you actually remember, and how much of it do you use daily, in real life? Of course we all need and still use the basics—reading, writing, science, history, and simple math. What about the other aspects of your interaction with teachers and peers? For some people, those years became a launching place into a successful career, while for others, it became the place of the greatest wounding to their self-esteem and the foundation for doubting themselves, God, authority figures, and the world around them.

Consider taking a personal inventory—what was your educational experience like? What did you learn to believe about yourself? About God? About those in authority and the world around you? What conclusions did you make, based on those educational experiences, that affected your choices and shape your life today? Most people are acutely aware of how their family life molded them into who they are, but what about the profound influence our years of education have on us? The years that we are most influenced and make our most important decisions are clearly from kindergarten through high school and college age. The God you now see is perhaps perceived cor-

rectly or incorrectly through the "glasses" you learned to see Him through during that time, but maybe not in the ways you might think.

As with all of the seven primary structures of society, education finds itself in perhaps it's greatest crisis ever, both in terms of process and end results. It's hard to know where to begin in describing the scope of its failures. As with the rest of culture, when you don't invite God into it, you are going to be in deep trouble. Among the major symptoms of its malaise, students are dropping out at record levels in the United States. Student test scores, when judged objectively, are the worst ever. Schools are plagued by underperformance of both students and teachers, with varying perspectives on who or what is to blame. Some teachers blame underfunding, some the curriculum, and others the students' behavior. Others blame class size. Many of the worst-performing schools are connected to areas of poverty and crime. Some say that racism in schools and hiring practices are worse than they have been in more than 50 years. Teachers are clearly demoralized by what is going on, and students are made to feel as if they are a statistical burden.

There is internal war over many aspects of the education system. For example, there is great debate as to which schools are better—conventional public schools or charter public schools. The documentary-style film *Waiting for Superman* by Geoffrey Canada detailed the failings of our educational system and suggested several repair strategies, beginning with the establishing of smaller charter schools. A group of teachers, sensing that public schools as a whole are under the gun, countered with a film called *The Inconvenient Truth Behind Waiting for Superman*. This film used their own opinions, studies, and surveys to argue that public schools are as good or better than the charter school options. There are ongoing discussions about the need for a culturally relevant curriculum rather than just ramrodding the same material that worked in previous generations. All in all, there are official and unofficial demands for an education reform movement. Many other nations are going through a similar crisis. Our educational structures don't just need a "Superman" but the One who is Superior to man—God the Teacher who is the source of all knowledge and wisdom. We need to see God as Wise Teacher in order to know how to make necessary changes to the way we teach in our systems of education.

What about the end result of those who do successfully make it through the education process? Are we really content with cookie-cutter citizens who are living the "American dream" of 40- to 60-hour work weeks, just to live under a pile of debt and have wealth and stuff that supposedly makes them happy? Is the goal of education to produce good people who make good money and do a few good things for other people? Or is the goal of education even to produce good Christians who make good money and do a few good things for other people? If God were to establish our education process His way, how would He do it? Would He insist on prayer, Bible classes, and Creationism?

Presently, that which passes for "education" doesn't have a clear direction or identity. It meanders in and out of three purposes depending where you experience it. The original purpose for education in America was to instruct and train in the ways of God as expressed through the Bible. Today it's also considered a tool for practical societal integration. This too has value and is more complex to pull off than it was 300 years ago. A third purpose seems to be laying the foundation for a person's career. To the degree it overemphasizes that point, it has strayed from the sphere of education to the sphere of business or economy. Rather than answering in this chapter all the challenges that relate to the educational system, we want more to present the color of God that shows His love through the paradigm of wisdom.

*We hope to convince you that the primary goal of education should be to connect us to our individual passion and the answers to the problems of that area of culture that we are interested in solving. It just so happens that God is the One with those answers. When education is done the way **God** teaches **us**, He doesn't even need to be directly spoken of in our public education systems. As with the other areas of culture, our assignment as those* *who know God is to take the aspects of His nature we have seen and display them as tangible love and practical solutions through every area of culture. Students will be connected to Him through their passion because they will eventually run up against problems that need His answers. When you have a positive educational experience that leaves the possibility of God's existence as an option, even if it's not taught, you encounter God's love as Wisdom. Let me explain ....*

LOVE DISPLAYED AS WISDOM

Soon after Johnny and I were married, I taught third grade at a private school for one year. I remember feeling so overwhelmed the first day as I looked at all those hungry eyes staring back at me in need of love. I knew I could never adequately give that kind of love to 25 of them seven hours a day, five days a week, for nine months. Knowing how needy and vulnerable I had felt at their age caused my heart to hurt for them—so little time to give them what they deserved, yet still more hours than even their own parents would have with them each day. What a responsibility and opportunity teachers have. Clearly the priority during those hours and years of education is to help each student gain specific knowledge about the world around them. But what about love?

In an ideal world, children will experience love from their parents while at home, but the majority of their awake hours are spent in a classroom setting. I don't believe growing in knowledge was ever meant to be experienced outside of the context of love. When we talk about the seven colors of love, what does love look like in the classroom? What does God as Love look like displayed in education?

Love seen in education looks like wisdom *and we have chosen the color* ***indigo*** *from the rainbow to represent it. Wisdom is an expression of love. In the same way that God not only loves us but* ***is*** *love, He is not simply wise but* ***is*** *wisdom. He doesn't just have all the facts, He knows what to do with them and wants us to know how to rightly apply what we know as well. True education doesn't just present facts and knowledge but provides an opportunity to grow in wisdom as well. Love is displayed in the context of* *education as wisdom. Wisdom is not simply experiencing how things work or knowing facts and truth. Wisdom is the understanding of when and how to apply facts, truth, and experiences.*

It's interesting that the color indigo on the color spectrum of the rainbow is right between blue and purple/violet—between the colors that represent religion and government. As a reminder, true religion (blue) is meant to reflect the heart of God as Redeemer, the One who has provided Jesus for our righteousness so we don't ever have to work or perform to earn an intimate relationship with God. And a healthy government (purple) not only protects our freedom to choose God but also maintains a safe and stabile environment that makes it easier for its citizens to believe God cares about them. God wants relationship with us so much that He protects our ability to choose Him, and when we do choose Him and invite Him in, He creates an environment that shows us how much He cares about us. Education, represented by that in-between color of indigo, is similarly a balance of these two realities. A learning environment must go beyond performance objectives alone and incorporate an atmosphere of care and concern for the students' well-being. The point of God as Wisdom and Teacher is that He loves you and He wants you to grow and mature. He loves you where you are, but He loves you too much to leave you there.

Education is the space in which the joy of the knowledge of God is fostered—not the knowledge of religion, but the understanding of what God is really like. True education produces a love for a lifestyle of learning. That doesn't necessarily mean that the subject of religion or God is talked about at school. When we speak of any truth, we are in essence talking about Him. He is the source of every truth and fact, the One who set all things and how they operate into motion. For example, when looking at a piece of artwork, you are learning about the artist, whether you realize it at that moment or not. When studying the truth about any subject, we are actually studying God because He is the One who made everything and sustains it all. Eventually our hearts catch up to this reality. Students may not even realize at the time that they are indeed growing in the understanding of God as they learn about His earth, and that's okay.

Wherever the reality of what He has made is presented without excessive pressure to perform and by authority that truly cares for the hearts of the ones learning, students will love learning, ultimately see God, and therefore grow in wisdom. When facts and knowledge about anything are presented correctly, it leaves us awed and inspired. When we are in awe of what God has created, we are basically in awe of Him, which the Bible says is the beginning of wisdom.[1] We don't always need to be told the obvious—that God knows everything, is the source of everything that's good, and understands how to apply all knowledge in ways that benefit us. When we're shown a correct perspective of simply what God is like, we can recognize Him for ourselves because it's wired into us to know our Creator when He is correctly displayed. For instance, whether a student is told that there is intelligent design to all of creation or not, it's quite obvious and instinctive to believe it when you learn about how flowers and bees work together, how the earth is the perfect distance from the Sun, and the amazing way our bodies work—unless you are told otherwise.

Learning about God and everything He created should be as exciting and creative as the world He made and the laws of nature He established. And where there's mystery, students should not have to create a "box" to attempt to fit it into. Wisdom acknowledges that we are not God and cannot understand or explain everything. If our education system limits itself to human understanding and our ability to rationally explain everything, then we're limiting God to be like us, which would make Him not God at all. Therefore, education must embrace the wonder and awe of a God and His creation that is much bigger than us or our ability to understand or express. Education systems that are healthy will allow room for the unexplainable as well as the rational and logical.

Just because we can't prove some things doesn't make them any less real. Education that doesn't come from that mentality is nothing more than facts and formulas given outside the context of love. Education that happens apart from love is dangerous because the recipients of cold facts will never

---

1   Proverbs 9:10

know how to apply knowledge. Applied knowledge or wisdom is the conduit for growth, life, and freedom. A lack of wisdom allows for knowledge to be used for destruction, death, and slavery. Think of all the technology we've advanced in—some has been used wisely to advance humanity, and some has been used without wisdom and has brought great harm to mankind. Education that has any value to it doesn't stop with information but will always lead to the knowledge of the One who made everything we are attempting to understand, the Wisdom of the Ages. Education disconnected from God is in fact atheist indoctrination.

THE LIE:
TRUE WISDOM IS SELF DEPENDENCE

Do you wonder what a world would look like if it were run by spiritual orphans—by those who believe that, if God exists, He certainly isn't looking after us very well? Well we don't have to wonder—take a look. We are in such a world, dominated by an education system that is centered around humanism. The dictionary defines humanism as "an outlook or system of thought attaching prime importance to human rather than divine or supernatural matters." Humanist beliefs stress the potential value and goodness of human beings, emphasize common human needs, and seek solely rational ways of solving human problems."[2]

Another word for humanism is "orphanology." The reason you've never heard that word is because I (Johnny) made it up! Consider this: humanism is the opposite of God-centered understanding. For those who have a humanistic way of thinking, humanity is the center of the world. They think that if God exists, He isn't relevant to real life, and only superstitious people believe in Him because they must need something to believe in for the hereafter. Bottom line, they live from a core conviction that they better be all they can be without Him.

---

2 Apple online dictionary

This foundational premise of humanism is now the basic toxin being intravenously fed to our children and young people, which is why I call it orphanology. I'll define it as the humanistic assumption that we have been left to figure out life without God. Orphanology creates spiritual orphans who are always in survival mode because they live from the perception that they have been abandoned and must hone their own survival skills. Since spiritual orphans don't recognize a Father's presence, they are continually in do-it-yourself mode. Their self-made structures will never have the foresight of a Father. Specifically, the way the education structure currently is perpetuates the lie that, if you are truly wise, you will depend on yourself and not God or anyone else.

This does not mean that effort is bad. Effort is an antidote to laziness, which I'm surely not commending. But when effort is not seen in the context of an existing and assisting Sovereign God, it has strayed into toxic effort. Effort is valuable to the degree it carries consciousness of a higher source—God.

Humanistic education celebrates what humanity has discovered and achieved. Wisdom goes beyond and celebrates the God who gave us the ability to discover what He made and the ability to achieve new levels of understanding His ways. Education that feeds the lie of self-dependence causes us to worship what we discover instead of the One who created it all to begin with. When we think life is all about us and believe we're the highest authority on any given subject, we also tend to think the natural laws that govern the earth are the highest laws. The problem with that thinking is that it simply isn't true. The God who made the laws of nature like gravity and weather patterns can supersede the laws He made because He's the One who made them. The things that seem the most concrete, rational, and factual to us are always at His mercy. The created is always subject to its Creator. God gives life and continues to sustain it, whether we choose to acknowledge it or not. Those who are wise have received the highest education of all by making a well-traveled path to the One we can depend on for the solutions to every problem and the answers to every question.

HOW DOES THIS LIE ABOUT GOD PLAY OUT IN CULTURE?

When we believe we're the only ones we can truly count on, the loneliness is profound. What begins as a theory becomes our reality. The collective ache is tangible throughout society. Every spare moment and dollar is spent trying to fill the distance we feel from the One we were never made to go through life without. We were not made to strive and scratch for everything we get in life. We were invited into a delightful dependence on a God who is more than enough for everything we don't have enough of. So we scramble and compete our way to our definition of success, wearing ourselves out and stepping on anyone who threatens our pursuit of happiness. Because we don't have any resources other than what we gather ourselves, we protect them at all costs, sometimes even at the expense of what really matters in life. We get an education for the purpose of living for what we can attain in status and material wealth but lose precious relationships, reinforcing the initial lie we were operating out of—that we can only depend on ourselves.

Others who embrace the lie of humanism play it out in another extreme as well. Rather than operating from a posture of "every man for himself," they turn to humanity as a whole to fill their need for help. In essence, they replace dependence on God or self with an unhealthy dependence on people. We have all done it to some extent, putting someone else who is only human up on a pedestal, hoping they can fill the need. Those who get desperate enough will throw away reason and caution, leaving them vulnerable to cult-type leaders and movements who promise what only God can deliver.

Self-dependence infuses culture through the education system by slowly convincing children that if they don't perform well and compete with their peers academically, their future isn't too hopeful. While it's certainly true that a good education is a big part of preparing for a good job, it definitely isn't a foolproof plan. Being able to memorize, understand, and communicate information doesn't guarantee anything. Even our next breath isn't guaranteed apart from God. The truth is, you can play the education game perfectly and still end up with a messed-up life. In the end, if your years spent studying do not teach you utter dependence on God, you most likely will stay stuck believing the false concept that your good grades and performance will get you acceptance, approval, and advance in life. That black-and-white, one-size-fits-all form of education promotes competitive, hierarchal, fight-your-way-to-the-top thinking that stays with you the rest of your life. That's knowledge without wisdom — information wrongly applied.

Healthy learning is not about performing for approval and acceptance and definitely not meant to happen in an atmosphere of fear and lack of care for the person. People are more important than information. The student getting the education is always more valuable than the education he's receiving. God gave us a world to discover because He loves us and wanted to give us more opportunities to know Him and what He is like, not because He planned on leaving us to figure it out ourselves as some survival game He could watch to amuse Himself. Self-dependence creates a climate where people serve knowledge rather than knowledge serving people. Self-dependence makes us wrongly believe that our performance in school secures our future and our ability to survive. In truth, it's God who sustains us and is the source of all wisdom. There's no greater ignorance than the inability to comprehend how dependent we are on God.

THE TRUTH:
TRUE WISDOM IS DEPENDENCE ON GOD

Did you ever play that game when you were little where you stiffen your body, cross your arms across your chest, close your eyes, and fall backwards into the arms of a friend who asks, "Do you trust me?" If we can help it, we will never depend on someone we don't trust. If you don't trust God, it's unlikely that you will allow yourself to fall into His arms. It's no surprise to any of us that it's extremely hard to learn to trust God. It's a heart skill that can take a lifetime to grow in.

*Let's name all the reasons we can think of **not** to trust Him: Every other authority figure in my life let me down or at least disappointed me, so why wouldn't He be any different? Surviving my years of education confirmed to* me that if I don't rely on my ability to work hard and figure things out, I will fail and become a failure. Trying to navigate the waters of my own sexuality and relating to the opposite sex, felt (or still feels) overwhelming and complicated—I definitely have had to figure that one out by myself. I have asked Him for help before and things still turned out bad. . . . . I'm sure we could all add to this list.

What about some reasons **to** trust Him? Every other authority figure in my life let me down and disappointed me, so maybe because He isn't like us, He's the only One who won't let me down in the end. In my process of getting an education, I saw how my best is barely enough in the big picture of life, and I can never know enough to not be in way over my head compared to where I wish I was. He knows everything, so why not go to Him for the answers to the problems of life and relationships? When I asked Him for help, maybe He did help me in ways I just couldn't see at the time. Where would I be if He didn't step in, in the way He must have?

Trust is built over time and with experience. You can have plenty of reasons to trust someone, but if you haven't recognized those reasons as they played out, then you won't rely on that person in the future. When we can see God in our past, we can see Him in our future.[3] Could it be possible that God never abandoned you or left you to survive without plans for something really good to come of it? Something so good that you may even one day be glad it turned out the way it did?

What I (Elizabeth) am going to ask you to do right now could be the most important moment of your life thus far and affect your future in ways that could be explosively freeing. Think back over your list of personal trauma, crisis, and tragedy. Now pick just one event that has been painful, devastating, or disappointing. Allow yourself to remember what happened and how it felt. In a moment, put the book down and close your eyes and let it replay in your mind's eye. But this time, ask God to show you where He was in the situation, what He was feeling about it and you, and what He was doing on your behalf. Ask Him to show you what He knew at that time that you didn't know

---

3   Another great quote from Bob Hartley.

and how that affected the situation and what you may have perceived as His lack of involvement. His arms were there to be strong for you, but sometimes we have to look hard to see them and even harder to feel them. But they were there. He never leaves us or forsakes us.[4] Look for Him. He was there.

Now for some, you may feel like He was there, but you wonder why in the world He let it happen, as if He could do nothing to stop it. Ask Him. If He is God, He is big enough to handle your questions. He wants you to know Him and His heart for you, so He can say it in a way that you can get it if you have a sincere desire to know the truth and to know Him. Trust His ability to speak in a way that you can recognize His voice in your heart. He can use your thoughts that sound an awful lot like your own inner voice to communicate with you. He can even use the screen of your imagination to show you a scene of the situation from His perspective, with the invisible spirit realm being seen in ways you couldn't see at the time.

God can give you all the reasons you need to trust Him if you're desperate enough to recognize Him in whatever ways He wants to show you. But be willing to expand your concept of how He speaks to you. It is rarely the way you think or prefer because He wants it to be real and not religious or stale. Maybe you need to forgive Him for how you felt He let you down in order to see Him and what He was actually doing on your behalf. Ask Him, and tell Him, until you feel your heart enlarge to the possibilities of His goodness. In that place, our hearts learn to handle the contradictions and mystery of how He is involved in our life. It always comes back to this: He works everything for our good, and our good is to know Him as He really is and not believe lies about who He is. Our good is to grow in the knowledge of God. Everything we go through is an opportunity either to believe a lie about Him or to learn a new perspective of what He is like and how much He loves and cares for us. Something that valuable will never come without great cost to us and without an adventurer's heart that's up for the challenge of a treasure hunt. He doesn't just provide a silver lining to our clouds; He's using those storms to accomplish important things in us. Sometimes He's teaching us to rest in

---

4   Deuteronomy 31:6, 8, Joshua 1:5, Hebrews 13:5

the midst of storms because it's so important for us to learn to trust Him, and then sometimes He's teaching us to use the authority and power He has given us to make the storms stop. Either way, in the end it's always about intimacy with God, where our heart begins to look at Him and realize it's all about Him, only to find Him looking back with His happy eyes that say, "I'm all about YOU!"

The treasure we are searching for behind everything is His goodness. He is reliable, trustworthy, and dependable for those who have the heart to recognize it. So fall. Fall into His arms. Fall into His strength that, like a magnet, draws out our weakness and doubts, only to consume them with His love. The truth is, only an education of the heart can graduate you from pain into the wisdom of complete dependence on God.

A sound education should instruct you that as you are diligent and simultaneously dependent, you can in fact rest assured that you will have a hopeful future. This becomes what love looks like through the eyes of wisdom. Responsibility, stewardship, and effort plus dependence on God assures a future. Wisdom validates effort only in the context of God awareness.

WHO IS GOD—AS TEACHER?

Jesus was called Rabbi, the Hebrew title used to express honor for a teacher. Jesus intentionally educated His disciples and everyone He spoke to for the three years He traveled and ministered town to town. As Rabbi or Teacher, Jesus' priority was to instruct them and later followers in the ways that Heaven functions. Jesus was sent by God to teach us what He is really like by the way He loved, served, healed, and spoke. Up until the time Jesus lived, the only perspective we had of God was hearsay, so to speak. With the exception of very few people, no one knew God directly or had long conversations with Him face to face. God is wise enough to know that even though you know something, you can't really relate to it until you experience it yourself. So God came in the flesh as Jesus and allowed Himself to experience what it's like to be an everlasting being like us and function within the boundary of a physical body with emotions and feelings born out of an earthly perspective. Jesus mastered the concept of dependence on His Father moment by moment. Even though He was the Son of God in bodily form, He looked to God as the Source for everything He needed to know, for all the power He used to heal, and for the strength He needed to trust God with on the path to the cross. When we look at Jesus, we see God as Teacher, among other things.

Have you noticed how the winners of American Idol and shows like that are usually people who have been singers their whole life? Many who don't win auditioned on a whim, having never really performed anywhere. They just had the idea it would be fun to become a recording artist. A true artist is one whether they ever get discovered or not. They write music and sing alone or in crowds because that's just who they are — an artist at heart. Jesus showed us by the way He lived that God is truly a Teacher at heart. God showed us through Jesus that He wants us to know and experience Him in every way. Jesus used every moment and situation as His classroom and recognized every conversation as an opportunity to instruct listening ears and hearts, not just in the ways of God, but in the heart of our Father.

Jesus showed us by the way He taught that God is an excellent Teacher. He used everyday examples of life to teach about profound truths. For example, He pointed to something as simple as a grape vine to describe the way we can connect with each other and with our Father. He took real life mundane events for that time period, like the washing of feet and the yearly feasts, to give meaning to new ideas He was cultivating in us. He spoke simply enough for children to understand but with enough mystery that we would value the end result of pursuing His ways. He knew when to talk about what so those listening could be prepared for the tests ahead. He not only used words but also modeled a lifestyle worth emulating. He taught by example, led by following, and called us into success by serving. Up until His last breath, Jesus made every move and spoke every word for our benefit so we might know what He knew — so that we might know the One He knows.

Think of the best teachers you ever had. Most likely you think of them for one of two reasons — they either truly cared about you, or they were passionate enough about what they taught that it provoked you to be inter-ested in that subject as well. That is God—as Teacher. It's not that God just thinks teaching us a lesson is a good idea. Rather, He deeply cares about us and has made truth and the discoveries of life available to us as another way to interact with Him and express His love for us. He also has an unending supply of passion for all that He created and set into motion. All of it is an outworking of who He is. True artists create because they love giving expres-sion to what they are, what they know, and what they see. They are excited to share it, not because they need attention but because they want others to receive something from it. God loves it when we not only learn to love like He does but also when we learn to enjoy what He enjoys. Why did He make sea creatures that we're just now discovering, and maybe even some that we'll never get to see? Why does He hide the most beautiful stones, the ones we refer to as precious, in the darkest of places? I think it's simply because wherever He is, He's there in all His creativity and beauty. He's every-where, so there's something to be discovered everywhere—high and low, in and out, giant and microscopic. God loves every topic and subject because He is every topic and subject. He doesn't just know everything; He's also the source of everything. To know His creation is to know Him. All truth is a potential onramp to the knowledge of God—the greatest education.

In the Bible, the book of Proverbs is filled with commendations and challenges to the reader to pursue wisdom, understanding, and knowledge. God is all about continuing education. Rumor has it that education will not cease in Heaven. (Remember how we talked about people who have died, been resuscitated, and now tell about what Heaven is like?) Some say that there will be a general knowl-edge of all things when we're in Heaven, but it will take eons of time to learn all the mysteries of the ages. They say those hungry to grow in knowledge will have opportunity to continue learning and that we're put through Heaven's version of schooling when we arrive. If there's anyone who knows how our education systems should func-tion, it's God, the Teacher of wisdom.

HOW CAN WE COOPERATE WITH GOD AS TEACHER
IN RESTORING WISDOM TO EDUCATION?

Education is in need of a big upgrade. What exactly needs to change? Wisdom—knowing what to do with what we know—must be restored to the process. Wisdom is an expression of who God is. As Teacher, He would never shuffle kids through a system like numbered cattle so He could check off the responsibility of having "educated" them. This Teacher cares so much about each one that His desire is for them to love learning and discovering truth, while finding their unique passion and gifts—applied knowledge. Only when we learn not just facts about our world but what our individual contribution to the world is have we truly been educated. Everyone needs to know their place and assignment or, no matter how many degrees they earn, they will never know their true value. Our value is a given, but discovering it is another thing. God as Teacher wants us as His students in the classroom of life to graduate knowing our profound value to Him. The thing we have the hardest time learning in life is the main reason we are here. You become convinced of your value when you realize that Someone as important as your Father, Creator, and God has given you an assignment.

*Our assignments are not what gives us our value. Rather, they are proof in our hearts that we have value. So the goal of this Teacher's system of education is to help His students grow in enough understanding of the world that they can find their passion and gifting, and then help them learn to access His solutions to the problems they were created to solve and needs they were created to meet. Many who believe in God have wrongly thought they had to work **for** God, but He invites us to work **with** Him in our assignment so we might grow in our relationship with Him and experience our value to Him. The goal of education is not to be smart or even position ourselves for a successful career. The goal of education is to discover our place in God's world and heart. As you discover your place in His **world**, your heart becomes acclimated to your place in His **heart**.*

God's love is seen as wisdom in the area of culture we call education. So how do we bring wisdom into our classrooms? Once education is put back on its original foundation, we have a reasonable bedrock from which to discuss the remaining challenges. We do need smaller class sizes, more resources, better teacher preparation and teacher benefits, better class discipline, more relevant curriculum, better public schools and private schools, better testing mechanisms, more sensitivity to race and economic impacts, and more. However, until we get the first thing first, this is like arguing about what kind of gravy we should put on rotten mashed potatoes. The foundation must be addressed, and the rest will follow. The foundation is God as Teacher. He is the Teacher, and all we, or the education system, needs to do is provide the essentials for discovery: a safe environment where students know they are prioritized over what they are being taught, teachers who enjoy the students and are passionate about their subjects, and freedom from extreme pressure to perform so that students love learning rather than dread it.

We can cooperate with God as Teacher by removing the sources of emotional and relational trauma in schools so children and young adults have the freedom to discover truth. Love and fear are opposites, like light and darkness. They cannot exist in the same space.[5] If we cared more about students feeling loved, accepted, and prioritized more than having them perform well on tests, they would indeed excel academically. All that God has made eventually points to Him, so we don't need to worry about His part. If we will simply give students a place to learn that is free from fear, God will engage their minds in a way that introduces Himself. He awakens their interests, passion, and purpose until they discover that what they are interested in was Him all along.

If you love patterns and numbers in math, so does He. If you love history and unique expressions in reading and writing, so does He. What if your interest in building and designing from a young age was Him all along? For those with a love for truth, all passions eventually lead back to the Source, back to God. He doesn't need our help. He isn't panicked because we aren't

---

5   1 John 4:18

making sure every child knows the Ten Commandments and prays before they eat their lunch. He's so much bigger than that. Even science leads us to the wonderful mystery of the Master Architect when taught truthfully (just the facts we actually know, not theories). You have to be told He didn't create everything in order to not believe in God as Creator. Wisdom, in the context of public education, gives the student the essentials for discovery, trusting God to reveal Himself. Ideally, parents are the voice and lifestyle demonstration at home of direct instruction about God.

It's safe to say that education has been hijacked from its original purpose. Until we get back to its original purpose, all other overhauls of the system will prove to be just cosmetic or, at best, statistical anomalies. The purpose of education is established in Proverbs 9:10: "The fear of the Lord is the beginning of wisdom, and the knowledge of the Holy One is understanding."

What does this mean in today's language? It means that the beginning of all learning starts with the premise that God is the center of the universe, and the first thing you need to figure out in life is what **His** rules for successful living are. This is His earth and His world and a child needs to know the "manufacturer's instructions" before he or she needs to know anything else. If you learn this, you have started on a path toward understanding.

The second part of the verse says, "the knowledge of the Holy One is understanding." This phrase makes more sense in the context of Rainbow God—the God of all of life. As we are expanding our perspective of who God is, our knowledge of God is increasing. Knowing the real Him apart from the lies we have believed about Him allows us to understand His heart and all He has made. Whereas before we might have thought only of a God of salvation and the hereafter, we now know of a God of the seven areas of culture that exist in every nation. Our increased knowledge of Him is designed to help us conclude that He really does have the better way of doing everything. He has better creativity and provision, better principles of media, better understanding of family, a better plan of salvation, a better plan of government, and a better education plan. In light of who we are seeing Him to be, it's inconceivable that we could believe that reading, writing, and arithmetic are the real foundations of learning.

Whether we have 10 students per class or 50, who cares what positive statistical blip is coming from that class if we aren't creating the right environment for students to arrive at their own conclusion of the centrality of God to all of life? It's missing the foundation of life. The foundation of life is that God IS. All other wisdom or instruction must build on that foundation. Every other foundation will ultimately develop a societal structure that will experience repeated systemic failures. Have you noticed that not one of the seven lead structures of society is working? Why not? Because the wisdom to formulate them has all come out of our present education systems. Our education system is responsible for reinforcing the philosophical assumptions of all the failed sectors of society. Who really cares if we get better scores—especially if the curriculum is founded on lies and half-truths? What does it do to the soul of a person to wrongly think that everything happened randomly by chance and their life began with no real intention? That soul is likely to live and die with no real intention, without knowing their assignment or value. In the big picture of life and eternity, who cares if you win at money and career but lose at the whole point of life—discovering how loved and valued you are? What does it do to a person's heart to wrongly believe that laws are created to keep everyone in line, but there are no principles and spiritual laws available for our success in career and in the bigger picture? They will never learn to live as ones who know Someone created them who has a desire to see them succeed and provided the guidelines to accomplish true success.

*Does that mean we have to preach God in schools? No, it means we have to be careful in schools not to undermine our children's ability to arrive at those correct conclusions on their own by teaching them false **theories** that crush their hearts and souls just because we believed the lie that we don't really matter. At some point, a generation of educators will stop that cycle* *in a way that does not infringe on people's right to choose religion. It is our responsibility to protect the student's freedom of religion by not imposing any particular faith, but we are attacking that right when we imply or teach things that cause the child to perceive faith as irrational and something that is just for those with no intellect.*

In the early history of the United States, Christians were the ones who established most schools and higher learning institutions. Clearly they had a value for the education and growth of individuals, as God does. We also know that those Christians had an equal value for the freedom of religion. They or their forefathers had experienced belief systems that were forced on them, and therefore they wanted to protect the rights of individuals to receive not only an education but one that doesn't force any particular religion on anyone. As we have stated over and over, God Himself values our freedom of choice even more than we do. He desires intimacy with us that is genuine and never forced, so how much more so should we who represent Him fight for the same?

Some Christians today seem to think that the ideal solution for our Education system would be to have the Bible as the foundation for all that is taught in every school, including public schools. Certainly we would all agree that we want our children to learn values, and we want our government to give us the freedom to provide private education based on any religion we choose. But we never want government to use the public school system as a way to promote any specific religion. Morality and relationship with God, yes. Legalism and religion, no.

You may wonder, how can education promote a relationship with God without promoting religion? How can education lead us to a conviction that God is central to all of life and that true wisdom is utter dependence on God — even while protecting freedom of religion? How do you allow for students to discover their own unique relationship with God as they are learning about their world without stepping over someone else's freedom to choose relationship with Him? The answer is the same for us individually, as well as in a school system. If we aren't going to impose religion on individuals, then why would we impose it in a classroom setting? Remember, any area of culture that reflects the way God is will ultimately be the best we could want.

God does not advance His kingdom or the knowledge of Him with some slick marketing campaign. He hasn't signed His name to one single thing He has created. He didn't make the truth of who He is obvious in the ways we would have liked for Him to.

*If God doesn't advance His kingdom by imposition, then we shouldn't do so in any way either. He wants us to know Him, so He must have a better way than the obvious to make Himself known. Think of yourself as an example—if you have an authentic and personal relationship with God right now, it isn't because of a religion you were taught. It's because you **experienced** His love. It may have been originally presented to you as religion, but you probably had to unlearn the religious aspect so that you could grow in actual intimacy with Him as your Father. So the point is, if the education system creates the same kind of freedom of choice that God does, while never undermining a child's natural wiring to believe in things they cannot always understand or explain, students will then be able to discover their purpose and be more likely to look to the One who can help them accomplish it.*

Overall, I (Elizabeth) think the public school systems in America are doing a pretty good job with maintaining freedom of choice in matters of faith. Some may disagree because of policies such as not allowing prayer in public schools. They feel we've gotten away from the original way that schools operated when the Bible was used directly for instruction, memorization, reading, and writing lessons and teachers prayed before food was eaten, etc. As good as it is to do those things, it clearly did not produce a harvest of spiritual or moral breakthrough generations later. Maybe we need to realize that government that protects students' freedom of religion is not the enemy in the war over education.

THERE IS ONE ENEMY IN THE WAR OVER EDUCATION

Remember the real enemy is Satan, the one who loathes God so deeply that he comes after His children with lies about their Papa, since the beginning from generation to generation. He distorts the face of God in our eyes so we won't trust God and give Him the desire of His heart—intimacy with us. Satan keeps us stuck in a rather simple cycle: we grow up believing lies about God ... we then perpetuate those lies through the culture that we have established ... which in turn acclimates the next generation to wrongly perceive God's heart towards them as well. Our culture is full of lies about who God is and who we are. We believe those lies because the difficult things we go through solidify our belief that God doesn't care. We do things our way (evidenced in our culture) because in our core we believe He doesn't care, which short-circuits the next generation's opportunity to experience culture that communicates and proves that He cares. This cycle can be interrupted, but we must first stop fighting each other and recognize the real enemy.

The face of the enemy in education is humanism, but beneath that is fear. Fear leads to humanism, which we have said is basically the belief that since we are alone we must be the center of our own universe and sweat and fight for everything we get. God values dependent effort, but humanism esteems independent effort. Humanism looks like pride, but beneath the pride is a core of fear. That fear instructs us that since we are alone, we had better prop ourselves up with at least a show of self-confidence. The enemy looks to use whatever education system we have in place, whether Christian or not, to enslave the next generation of God's sons and daughters to fear. Fear has many ways it touches students, from anxiety over being accepted to the fear of failure. Where fear is, there is no experience of love, and where there is no love, there is no wisdom (learning and applying what we learn to our future). Fear leaves you in survival mode with no energy left to discover things like your dreams and passions that can help change the world. Where there is no wisdom, no one is really being educated beyond simply memorizing facts.

The war over education has a lot to do with God, but not in the ways many Christians think. The war is not with government over prayer in schools or teaching creation versus evolution. The war is over the basic idea that there is obviously a big picture of life around us that has pattern, design, structure, and laws that we are a part of, but that we did not start ourselves, nor do we sustain it. Like the war that goes on in each of our individual hearts, this war over education was initiated by Satan as an attempt to keep us from knowing

God. Government is not the enemy as long as it remains within the fine line of protecting the freedom to choose God by not teaching or forcing religion or undermining a student's choice by directly or indirectly belittling the hard-wiring for faith that they were born with. We must not allow the enemy to use broken and disappointed people who have not found their own faith and expanded understanding of God and His goodness to dictate education laws or classroom topics that steal faith from the next generation.

The enemy in the war over the education of our children has a goal to strip every child of hope—the anticipation of God to be good in their life and in the world. Look at the faces of just about every graduation class. You'll see little hope and lots of fear disguised with either plans for shallow living, selfish ambition and gain, or a naive idea that they can change the world without God's solutions. Satan has had us locked down, generation after generation, believing we can educate our children to depend on themselves and then somehow grow up to make the world better. We have tried for a while now, and it is obvious that we simply cannot do it without God. But He will have the last word, like He always does when we invite Him in.

THE HOPEFUL FUTURE FOR EDUCATION

Many Christians in the United States feel that the main change needed in public education is to get prayer and the Bible back into schools, similar to our early history when we were primarily made up of Puritans and Quakers. Even speaking practically, which one of the over 30,000 denominations would get to promote their particular slant of the Bible? Which prayer style would teachers invoke? Would they pray in tongues to accommodate the Pentecostals and Charismatics? Or would more conservative prayers like those of Baptists be best? Should the students be taught to pray to the Father, Son, or Holy Spirit? And what if little Johnny (no pun intended) grew up being taught you can only pray to one of them? What brand of creationism would be taught? Seven literal days or seven figurative days?

I (Elizabeth) am hopeful about the education system, but not because I foresee official Christianity taking over the schooling of the next generations. If we were to do that, given the current Christian mentality—get God into the classroom by teaching the Bible, prayer, and creationism—then I believe we would find ourselves fighting God, not government. When we don't do things His way, we are fighting God because He fully intends to free us from everything that is not His heart, including religion. The future is bright for education because it's becoming more obvious that what we're doing isn't working, which opens us up for necessary change. We will learn to partner with God's way of teaching by aligning our education style with His education style—an atmosphere of freedom of choice and freedom from fear. The atmosphere of His heart leaves us filled with hope, knowing our worth and assignment, and knowing we are cared about even more than the facts that we are being taught. Wouldn't classrooms that reflect that be amazing? It almost makes me want to go back to school. Almost.

Picture classrooms and graduating classes full of students who aren't so burnt out emotionally and academically that they can't wait to be done. Imagine students who love to learn so much that they never stop because they embrace learning as a personal lifestyle. Dream with us about schools filled with kids and young adults who are taught by teachers who genuinely care about the students and are empowered to present their subjects in the most exciting way possible. Wouldn't it be amazing to send your kids and grand-kids to a place that allows them to learn the basics as a means to a greater discovery of what they are gifted and uniquely wired for? Think about how much more impact teachers could have on their students if they were given the opportunity to expose them to rich studies without pressuring them all to perform the same way, just to meet certain statistics.

Obviously all kids need the basic levels of reading and math, but early on children should be drawn into something that keeps their attention and curiosity. If school doesn't feel exciting and safe, then something else in their life that's more important than school may need to be addressed. Or maybe what or how we are presenting to students is not worth their attention. We will eventually address the wrong philosophy of trying to make everyone the same by strengthening their weak areas. What if we further strengthened the areas they are already good at and helped them excel? Some schools are already doing that to some degree, but what if we were able to shift the system enough to have that process begin at a very early age, while they still enjoy learning and thinking creatively, rather than thinking only linearly? Won't it be great to have children running in the door after school, thrilled to tell about what they learned? And waking up early because they can't wait to get back to a place where they feel loved and accepted because they are good at what they are passionate about? We put man on the moon. Surely we can accomplish that.

We are hopeful about education for the same reason we are hopeful about all the other areas of culture. God has a glory of education that is yet to shine. His true colors of love will fill the whole earth, including this deep blue/indigo color. The glory of who He is in every area of society will be known throughout the earth. His sons and daughters will arise and take the challenge of restoring His correct reputation as the God of all of life. They will see their opportunity to co-labor with a great God and bring amazing innovations to another failed sphere of society. These kids of God as Teacher will create brilliant new school models. They will develop right-brain learning curriculum that students will love because it connects them to their hearts and not just their heads. There will be idea after idea and innovation after innovation. This is the advantage of co-laboring with God. He is an inexhaustible source of all of His attributes. Because of this, it all starts with inviting Him in and volunteering to partner with Him. Whether it's easy or not, those who do will not be alone. What a privilege to live in such a day and time. Everything is about to radically change.

INVITE HIM IN—AS TEACHER

*In the fifth line of "The Lord's Prayer," Jesus prayed, **"Give us this day our daily bread."** I (Elizabeth) love the way this connects to education and God as Teacher in an unexpected way.*

As we write this book, our daughters are ages 11, 15, 18, and 21. We are about halfway through our grand adventure of raising them. The year I taught third grade was the year I got pregnant with our first. Looking back, I realize that the pain I had stuffed from my childhood, along with the fear of entrusting my kids to someone else, fueled our decision to home-school our kids. Honestly, if I had it to do over again, I would not have home-schooled them because I created an atmosphere in our "classroom" exactly the same as what needs to change in the education system I was trying to save them from. I was so afraid that they would not choose a relationship with God and me that I attempted to control their environment. In retrospect, I understand now that I simply didn't know God well enough to trust Him with my kids. Since I was home-schooling them I also felt a pressure to prove that they were getting a good education, so I made learning about performance. If parents are an aspect of the face of God to their children, then I showed them a God who is worried about them and not sure that He can maintain their hearts and desires without being overwhelmed. For us, home-schooling was no better than another school because I showed them a wrong perspective of God by my fear and control. I'm also sure that most of the time they felt like what I was teaching them was more important than they were, which is far from God's heart towards them. I often remind them that at least they learned to forgive a lot! One thing we have done well so far is to help them find and practice their passion. The thing that was missing for me is what's missing in most school settings, whether public, private, or home school: we must learn to invite God in as Teacher.

*When we invite God in as Teacher, it takes the burden off us and allows us to do what we ultimately want our kids to learn to do. We want them to secure their future by fully living in the moment and look to God as the source for everything they need. When we live in the moment, we aren't worried about the future. I'm not saying to be irresponsible and live **for** the moment, but to live in it. When we are fully alive to our heart and to God's heart, we aren't in survival mode. When we aren't in survival mode, then we can think, create, and process things clearly and access God's heart and solutions for the problems around us. When we aren't consumed with fear, we can be* *passionate without reacting to things we're afraid of. When we're full of hope because we're standing next to a God who is huge in our eyes, then we aren't afraid of the future and can actually plan well for it — not just our own little future, but the future of whatever area of culture we are drawn to. We look at our niche of passion as a way to give and not take, which becomes a reward far more precious than personal gains in career and wealth, but usually ends up producing both.*

Jesus mentioned bread as He taught and used it several times as a significant "show and tell" lesson for His students. For example, at least twice He supernaturally multiplied a few loaves to feed thousands.[6] When Jesus went into the desert for forty days to fast and pray to prepare Himself for ministry, He was tempted by Satan to turn stones into bread. As hungry as He was, He resisted by quoting scripture from the Old Testament: "Man doesn't live by bread alone, but by every word that God speaks." [7] Right before He died, Jesus also took the bread from a yearly feast the Jews called Passover and spoke of Himself as the Bread of Life that would be broken for us. He encouraged all who follow Him to also eat bread and drink wine together in remembrance of Him until He returns to earth.[8] (Of course we call that communion.) And we also know that in Biblical days, bread was a staple of their diet and part of their daily sustenance. So when we read His prayer, "Give us this day our daily bread," He is inferring quite a bit.

Jesus is instructing us to ask for what the moment requires, and in that, our perspective of Him expands and becomes more accurate. When we ask for daily bread, we are in essence acknowledging that He holds the future and is what sustains our present. We are living from wisdom by being utterly dependent on Him.

The thousands who needed the loaves of bread to be multiplied had two needs: to learn about the Father and to eat. Jesus knew how to feed them in a way that satisfied their immediate hunger and unforgettably demonstrated what our Papa is like. When He stated that we don't live on food alone but

6   Mark 6:30-44, 8:1-10
7   Matthew 4:4
8   1 Corinthians 11:23-26

*actually on what God speaks to us, He was pointing us to the One who sustains us daily, moment by moment. As Jesus spoke of Himself as bread that is broken for us, He was making clear to us, in terms we could understand, that it is His life given for us that nourishes or feeds us. Each mention of bread has many layers of truth built into it, but all point to the **wisdom** of looking to God daily rather than to ourselves.*

God is not the circumstance that you're going through or the sad story you've lived through, nor should He be defined by it. He is the One who comes into the mess of it and helps you learn to find Him above the voice of the enemy, who shouts his lies that God is the One to blame. God is not the pain that you're in, but He is the remedy for it and the One who is using it to prepare you for an eternity of everything you have been desperate for. Invite Him in as the Teacher who is ever speaking words of wisdom and instruction so that you pass the tests and graduate into His fullness. Invite Him in as the Teacher who will always take you to the Source for every daily need—the Teacher who is fervently committed to your graduation into all that He is, which is more than we can imagine or hope for. He is God, your Teacher, and He knows just how you learn best. He knows all the different learning styles that we have, and He knows yours. So trust Him. Keep your natural and spiritual senses wide open, and be sure to take notes along the way. You never know who you may be able to help pass their tests in life too.

CHAPTER EIGHT

PROVIDER: The Color of Riches
THE SOLUTION FOR OUR ECONOMIC SYSTEMS

Money, like God, is something everyone has a relationship with, whether they acknowledge it or not. Our relationship with money is unique to the way we were first introduced to it, how much or little interaction we have had with it, and our future plans for it. Some learn to live without it, while others are dying with it. Americans have engraved their pledge of trust in God on it but live in fear and stress when it's hard to find. Once again, we want to challenge you to confront your current relationship with money and see if your perspective of God as your Provider may need expanding.

LOVE DISPLAYED AS RICHES

*In the context of **economy**, we chose the color **green** to represent God as the **Provider** of **riches**. Green not only makes Americans think of the dollar and prosperity but also the life of new plants in the spring that begin to overtake the death of winter. Green speaks to us of something that is healthy and vibrant. Of course in recent years, the expression "Go Green" reminds us to value the life and resources on our planet enough to conserve them. Our Provider is the source of all we value and of life itself. Green is another color of His love that our economy could use more of.*

*God's love is so limitless that it overflows everywhere things are done **His** way. For those who have hearts to let Him in, there's always plenty of love. When economy is done God's way, His love overflows as riches, and there's plenty to go around. We have seen God as love overflow in family as Papa, in religion as Redeemer, in government as King, in media as Communicator, and in education as Wisdom. His love in our economic culture overflows as God our Provider. What does God provide for us? Nothing less than the riches of His love. **Love looks like riches when displayed in a nation's economy.***

*God's love is meant to be displayed as riches, or the abundance of resources, through our economy. When the world economic system is functioning at peak performance, we will know it because there will be no lack. To the degree love is poured out as practical resources and basic needs, we can know God is involved in our economy, whether it's our personal, national, or global economic status. His heart is moved by what enslaves us—our poverty, as well as our greed. His love searches out all the things that keep us from knowing **Him** as Provider, and when we get His heart, we will do the same for others.*

As important as money and economy are for obvious reasons, the main reason they are important is because they are yet another aspect of who God is and another opportunity to know and interact with the real Him. What does God think about money and economic structures of nations? Does it matter to Him whether you or your nation has plenty or lives in poverty? If you think He does care, then why do you think so? In your mind, is it because He wants to punish or reward you? Or because He thinks you have or haven't worked hard enough to earn it? If you are one who thinks that God doesn't care about your financial situation, maybe it's because you believe He has left you on your own to figure it out—again, like a spiritual orphan. What you believe about money reflects what you believe about God. And what you believe about God is reflected in what you believe about money.

What we collectively believe about money is played out in our economic system, which is clearly failing. We have been hearing warnings for years and years about the economy crashing, but since August 29, 2008, we have had clear evidence of a world economic crisis that continues to reverberate. The leading financial experts have seemingly all offered their best solutions, yet nothing has worked. Certain indexes have improved, but a frighteningly overwhelming debt threatens our very way of life. No one's economic projection is good, and many are simply terrifying.

The fact that the world's economic system is failing doesn't mean all economies will fail; it just means the present system is failing. The failing system is based on assumptions that have been conclusively proven to be wrong. Some assumptions are at individual levels, and some assumptions are at national levels. There seems to be an honest attempt to find the right way to have a balanced, vibrant economy, but if we don't identify the systemic failures, we won't do much better moving forward.

All failed economic systems are founded on philosophical fallacies. These are ideas that have a future destruction sown into them from their conception. The two most impacting failed ideas in the economic area of our culture are: If you want to make money, you have to love money; and if you want to have more money, you must save more money. These two foundational thoughts feed a central lie about God that we are all tempted to believe, especially in these days.

THE LIE:
IT IS POINTLESS TO TRUST GOD FOR RESOURCES

The first failed idea is the belief that if you want to make money, you have to love money. The old King James version of the Bible addresses this idea by telling us that "the love of money is the root of all evil."[1] Other translations say that actually means the love of money is the root of all kinds of evil. Either way, it still isn't good. Loving money may fuel a person's drive to make money, but in the end it's dangerous. So why is the love of money such a problem? This

1   1 Timothy 6:10

is a very relevant question that goes to the heart of the matter. One of God's names is Jehovah-Jireh, which means, "The Lord is Provision." He not only provides; He is actually provision itself.

God doesn't have to have a financial plan or generate a fundraiser among the millions of angels in heaven. He simply speaks, and provision is forthcoming. God's spoken word itself generates whatever He needs. In the beginning, He didn't have to draw up plans for earth and discuss them with His board of archangels. He didn't need a plan of implementation. He just needed to say, "Let there be," and there was. He generated a world economy in seconds. He said, "Let there be energy," and there was energy. He called it Light. He said, "Let there be food for everyone," and there was. He called them fruit-bearing trees and plants. He said, "Let there be water for everyone and everything," and there was. Finally, He made man from the dust of the earth, and we are still here and now number over seven billion. God didn't have to dig, sweat, strategize, leverage, stress, plan, toil, synergize, fill out papers, get a credit check, apply for a loan, call His rich uncle, borrow from His parents, or sell His stock shares. He just said, "Let there be," and there was.[2]

So why is the love of money so wrong? The reason is that it's fed by the lie that if you have money, you can buy everything else you need. The follow up assumption is that with money, you can be all you want to be. People wrongly assume that they can be wealthy, famous, and live in great comfort if they have enough money. All we need to do is read the daily newspaper about the latest celebrity who committed suicide to realize that this presupposition is wrong. Money can buy a lot of things, but it cannot buy love, joy, or peace.

The irony here is that God is not asking us to be poor or even to hate money. The Source of all provision is literally able to produce billions out of thin air. Furthermore, being a good Father, He enjoys providing for His kids. He doesn't just begrudgingly provide for us, but

2 Genesis 1

He delights in being our Provider. Therefore when we don't look to Him for what we need, it's the ultimate insult to who He is. When you are the Source and your kids love money and look to it more than to you, you know you have a foundational problem of trust. Our goal in life with regard to our personal finances is to live out the statement, "In God we Trust." I (Johnny) don't want to just read it on my dollar bill; I want to actually eat, live, and breathe that reality daily. When I look at a dollar, I remember it isn't my source. The One who provided it is.

The other failed idea is the belief that, if you want to have more money, you must save more money. Now this idea seems to make common sense, but riches cannot be dealt with by common sense. I'm not talking about having some responsible level of emergency cushion in your bank account, but more of the false concept that storing up brings increase of riches. Riches are intrinsically wired to our hearts and spirits. We've all heard Jesus' wise words about money, "Where your treasure is, there your heart will be."[3] That means there's a hook in your money that is connected to your heart. Wherever you put your money, your heart's energy and passion will follow. If you have a lot of money in savings, your concern will be there. If you have a lot of money in stocks, your focus will be there. If you have a lot of money in your car or house, your heart's affection goes there. In effect, your money steers your heart. What a powerful reality! That's why Jesus advised us, "Lay up treasures for yourself in heaven."[4] This means we should invest in heavenly causes—in the things that mean something in the context of eternity.

Jesus even more pointedly speaks to that when He says:

> "...Do not worry about your life, what you will eat or what you will drink; nor about your body, what you will put on. Is not your life more than food and the body more than clothing. Look at the birds of the air, for they neither sow nor gather

---

3   Matthew 6:21
4   Matthew 6:19-20

into barns; yet your heavenly Father feeds them. Are you not of more value than they?" [5]

God implores us to see the green color of His love for us. In essence, He's telling us that if we'll let Him, He'll take care of us. We really can trust Him. He even takes care of the birds of the air that have to figure out the provision thing every day. If He takes care of them, how much more will He take care of us who are of more value to Him?

A quick story to reiterate the power and intimacy of what God is saying to us: A few years ago, the night before we were going to take our daughter off to college for the first time, I (Elizabeth) was feeling that panic that so many other moms have felt when they have to learn to let go and trust God with their children. I was singing a song that says, "I know, if Your eye is on the sparrow, then Your heart is on me." [6] I began to talk to God about how I was feeling and asked Him if it was in fact true that He knows and cares every time even a little sparrow falls. The next morning, I woke up before everyone else, with a sense of dread about the day. When I went downstairs to get breakfast, I was greeted by a real sparrow sitting on the floor, inside our house, at the foot of the staircase! It must have fallen in through one of our chimneys, but never before or since has that happened. God was answering me loud and clear. He cares more than we even hope for about everything that concerns us, because of our great value to Him.

Jesus went on to say: "Therefore do not worry, saying, 'What shall we eat?' or 'What shall we drink?' or 'What shall we wear?' . . . For your heavenly Father knows that you need all these things."[7]

Then He gives us the great balancing word on the whole subject: "Seek first the kingdom of God and His righteousness, and all these things will be added to you."[8]

---

5   Matthew 6:25-26
6   "Embrace" from the album "Marked by Heaven" by Jake Hamilton—great music!
7   Matthew 6:31
8   Matthew 6:33

God the Provider's plea to us is not unreasonable. He's basically saying, "Listen, I know all the stuff you need. I am the God of the real world, not just the God of spiritual things. What I need from you is to think of my kingdom first." Remember that when we talk about God's kingdom, we are not talking about some arrogant man's need to rule. The kingdom is the King's way of doing things — the King's culture of love that is seen in Heaven and one day will be seen in our culture too. As we seek or search out God's better way of doing things and display His love through all areas of life, then what we personally need really will be taken care of.

It is not that we shouldn't have savings accounts, stocks, cars, or houses. We should be heavily invested enough in kingdom activity, in those things that reflect His true heart, that more of our heart is connecting to God than to our investments. In fact, when we make investments intentionally thinking first of His kingdom, we really start getting on the right page with Him.

You may wonder why so many people are impoverished and starving in the world. The answer is less complicated than you might think and one that we are consistently reiterating. God shows up where He is invited and where room is made for Him. Our world is full of those with orphan mentalities and great needs in every area of life because we have tried to make it without Him. We assume He has abandoned us and therefore look to other sources, wondering why it looks like He has abandoned us. In the story of the prodigal son who ran away from his father's home, it was the son who left the father and therefore was barely surviving eating the pigs' food. The father was daily waiting for his prodigal son to return so that He could joyfully fund and feed him.[9] This is still how our God thinks and operates. He wants us to know that if we will think of Him and the way He does things first, then He will be our Source. If you keep looking only to yourself, you are going to regularly find yourself under resourced. Ignore God as Provider and you will end up in the pigpen of life.

---

9 Luke 15:11-32

Most of us need a healed perspective of God in this area of provision. Even most Christians I (Johnny) know carry an orphan perspective about their finances and the overall economy. I myself get buffeted with that mentality from time to time. An orphan mentality is no dig on orphans themselves, for they are worthy of great sympathy, attention, and help. But the orphan way of thinking is a distorted way of perceiving God. It causes us to forget that God is still God, not only in heaven but on earth, in every nation and in all aspects of society. True trust in God is more valuable than a billion dollars in gold coins hidden in your back yard. You can't define trust in terms of an amount of money, investments, or other safety nets. Trust is like a delicate flower that you must nurture and intentionally give attention to. I know from experience that when the flower of trust doesn't wither, it produces the fragrance of love, peace, and joy. It far exceeds the comfort of a high net worth or a cushiony bank account.

So when we realize we're relating to money from these wrong assumptions, we're able to overcome the lie the enemy whispers to convince us that it's pointless to trust God for resources. It's never pointless to turn to God as Provider because He delights in pouring out all that is His to those who look to Him.

HOW DOES THIS LIE ABOUT GOD
PLAY OUT IN CULTURE?

When we don't believe we can trust God for what we need, we revert back to what we unfortunately learned in school—depend on yourself and don't count on anyone else. With that mentality comes a whole skill set of using and climbing over anyone necessary to make your way to success. Individuals do it and corporations do it. The unspoken rules are the same, and the eyes become trained to see others as a means to an end and definitely not the way God sees us or desires us to see one another.

A recent CNN headline story is a great example of how this lie about God plays out in the current economic culture. "Goldman Exec

Quits, Calling Firm Toxic,"[10] executive Greg Smith was quoted as saying, "I can honestly say that the environment is as toxic and destructive as I have ever seen it." Interestingly, his central complaint is that the company cares more about making money **from** its clients than making it **for** them. He then describes the internal bragging of managers who acknowledge ripping off their clients. His last quote stated, "It astounds me how little senior management doesn't get a basic truth: If clients don't trust you they will eventually stop doing business with you. It doesn't matter how smart you are."

What a statement! From the top of the economic food chain an executive identifies that trust is the real currency. This is, of course, what has locked down our present economy. There isn't enough trust to do business. Banks don't trust people. People don't trust the government. Government doesn't trust banks. There's a trust deficit in all directions because ultimately the cure for it all starts with horizontal trust. Whoever was responsible for getting the "In God We Trust" declaration on our money really seems to have understood that all lasting financial wellbeing comes from the Man in Green—God our Provider, God our Source.

God's currency is TRUST, and the enemy's currency is FEAR, GREED, or both. If you find your daily realities being more in the fear/greed camp, then make the necessary adjustments. Trust isn't easy, but it's necessary. Sometimes you have to stare down your fear and eyeball it face to face and declare to it and to yourself that you trust God the Provider. God is not fragile, but our trust can be. One bad day for Wall Street and our confidence can come crashing down. We have to cultivate trust in our relationship with God, just like we do in any important relationship in our life.

As you put the trust and fear/greed priorities in order, you can begin to properly structure your vocational life. What doesn't make sense is to spend 30 years doing something you hate doing. Your

10 March 14, 2012

work is supposed to be your life's calling. What you do day in and day out is meant to line up with a servant-hearted passion. I add the word "servant" because it may be someone's passion to "be famous" as an end in itself, but that's a self serving passion as opposed to something that will ultimately give you the impact you were created to have. You can only find your purpose and fulfillment when you are sincerely motivated to make the world a better place. Wisdom will then tell you that the world can only be a better place if one of God's true colors is shining through you. You want to find the colors of God that reflect what's in your heart and then re-present Him to others through His way of changing and influencing that area of culture. You were made in His image and called to reflect that image. Your vocation or work is the exchange of finances for service provided. Your ultimate goal in business should be to be so passionate about the humanitarian value of what you do, that your work life reflects an image of God. Millions and millions of His sons and daughters are about to get this like never before, and the riches of our economy will be restored. There is a glory as to how God provides and the whole earth will be full of that glory.

THERE IS ONE ENEMY IN THE WAR OVER ECONOMY

Again, we must point out that there a war is going on in this sector of society, as with all areas of culture that were originally intended to show us the true colors of our Rainbow God. Satan as Mammon shows up on this battlefront with a simple strategy: He uses his influence and lies to get people to trust in money rather than in God. He gets us out of balance in one way or another, either by pushing us to pursue money too much or to settle in to poverty. Satan will actually help us make money to keep us always wanting more. He enslaves us to fear over losing everything, provoking us to hoard in case of a disaster. He does whatever it takes to keep us stressed, worried, and always focused on money. We end up disconnected from trusting in our mega-zillionaire Papa, convinced that money is **the** key for whatever future we desire.

Mammon is doing a pretty good job of perpetuating the lie that it's pointless to trust God for what we need. Jesus spoke of the deceitfulness of riches,[11] or its ability to captivate us. He also warned us that Mammon wars for the very seat of God in our life.

"No man can serve two masters; for either He will hate the one, and love the other; or else he will hold to the one and despise the other. You cannot serve God and Mammon."[12]

Mammon competes for the place of preeminence in our life. When we give ourselves permission to be lovers of money, we set ourselves up to resent God. When we find our security in our bank account, we make that our trust fund rather than making God the Provider our trust. No matter what financial gain you attain, if it lessens your trust in God, it's your enemy and not your friend. Many of us require a daily recommitment to God in this area with some practical proofs such as giving first to God and then becoming committed to ongoing generosity with the rest.

HOW CAN WE COOPERATE WITH GOD AS PROVIDER IN RESTORING RICHES TO ECONOMY?

God the Provider is looking for co-laborers to be able to handle the immense wealth that He has made available for those who are prepared to show the world how much He loves them. I know just a handful of these and have been privileged to hear how they are thinking and functioning with wealth. They have a "be a channel"

11 Matthew 13:22
12 Matthew 6:24

mentality rather than a "dam up the resources" mentality. They don't just make a goal for how much income they can accumulate; their primary goal is to see how much they can give away. One who already gives millions once said to me excitedly, "God has asked me to believe I can give billions!" He never mentioned making billions, just giving billions. When your mind and spirit operate in that kind of thinking, you are positioning yourself to be greatly trusted by God the Provider—the One who can produce green out of thin air. This man didn't stop to think about the fact that to give billions you have to make billions. He was just excited about the opportunity to be a giver at this level and was eagerly preparing his heart for such a time. He has been faithful first with thousands, then ten thousands, then hundred thousands, and now millions. God cannot trust you with an overflow if you've shown an inability to be faithful with little. If you ignore Him when you handle hundreds, don't expect Him to trust you with much more. You may attain wealth, but it will come with much sorrow.[13]

In the coming days, God will have authentic "ministers of wealth." These will be people who think of being channels and not dams. A dam is a hoarding mechanism designed to stop the flow. Being a channel may mean the person has very modest personal financial flow but is a conduit for great provision to flow through them for others. Even many charitable givers are dams first, and then give out of that abundance, always maintaining a dam full of personal resources. I won't knock them or that strategy, but I will just say that those whom God as Provider will trust with billions and even trillions will be those who are happy to operate as channels even at their own risk. They will have such a profound trust relationship with God that they will always know more is forthcoming. God the Provider is an inexhaustible source, and we are going to see that in amazing ways in the days ahead. So much needs to be done with these massive amounts of

---

13 Proverbs 10:22

resources, but God has to be very selective with powerful riches that can steer a heart. Those who position themselves as channels of His resources have a heart that continually comes back to God because that is where their treasure has been going—towards the issues that touch His heart. Those who are dams for resources constantly wrestle with where their heart is.

THE HOPEFUL FUTURE FOR ECONOMY

God will begin to use His children in countless ways in the coming days. It all starts with recognizing who He is and inviting Him in. All who want to serve as an extension of His provision on earth are invited to participate. He doesn't require you to be perfect or have a high paying job. You may never be able to build enough trust in Him to administer billions, but maybe you can handle hundreds or thousands. You can start where you are and see what you are able to grow into. Our currency is a simple trust in God that is earned as we learn to be faithful in the little. As you establish your identity as one who seeks first His kingdom with the small amounts you steward over, then you can then grow into greater measures of stewardship of riches that bring a blessing to the giver and the receivers.

God has so much to do on planet earth, and all of it will require extreme wealth. Almost everything He does is in conjunction with His children who understand their roles as ambassadors of His kingdom. God has cities and nations to rebuild, disease and famine to eradicate, and issues of justice to resolve. The need for emergency relief funds will be an increasing reality in the future, as the earth's birth pangs create more and more earthquakes, tsunamis, tornados, storms, and severe weather patterns. Most of what we think of as judgments from God are simply that region of the earth crying out for help. Often it's because that area is laden with the sin of that city or region, but it usually still isn't God's judgment. Creation itself cries out for the sons and daughters of God to show up with the fullness of who He is and how good He is.[14]

There is no economic crisis on earth that God has not already placed the solution for in His sons and daughters who are willing to co-labor with Him. There is no economic crisis that will ever come that He won't already have the solution for, available through His kids. We simply need to awaken to who He is and what He is all about and then arise and shine with what He has given us. We must become convinced that we have never been orphaned on planet earth, no matter how much it may feel that way at times. God knows the things we need, and He has given us the parameters of how we are to receive His abundant provision in a way that it won't harm us. He gave us clear instructions to seek His kingdom first, and then He will give all that's needed to us and through us. The current economic crisis isn't hopeless. The present U.S. debt of multiple trillions only **seems** impossible to deal with. There's already a plan available to reduce it to nothing. This plan will come through His sons and daughters who are co-laboring with Him and have positioned themselves to be ministers of His heart on earth. I am not talking about ordained ministers of church, but people who know the real Him and are ready to make the real Him known.

Just how hopeless can any financial picture be when an eager and willing God is available to interact and relate with? Our massive economic troubles are just one "Let there be" away from being resolved. He won't intervene unwisely or prematurely, as we do have to make some adjustments, but don't think for even a moment that a practical solution straight from His heart doesn't exist.

---

14 Romans 8:19

THE TRUTH:
GOD ENJOYS PROVIDING FOR US AND THROUGH US

*A few years ago, we went to see the Broadway production of "Joseph and the Amazing Technicolor Dreamcoat," the musical based on the biblical account of Joseph.15 For those who aren't very familiar with the Bible, this is not the same Joseph who was married to the mother of Jesus. This Joseph lived many generations before that and went through years of betrayal, slavery, false accusation, and imprisonment as a process of preparation to partner with God in saving the people of Egypt from starvation during a seven year famine. It's quite a story in many ways, but my favorite thing about this historical account is what it tells us about **God**. He truly desires to show us what He is like and how much He cares about us, if we care enough to perceive it.*

Joseph's father gave him a coat of many colors when he was a boy, and that made his brothers very jealous. Evidently this coat was valuable because of the many colors. Joseph's brothers then threw him into a pit and sold him as a slave. His master whom he had served faithfully, then ended up imprisoning him on false charges. While in prison, he served other prisoners by using his relationship with God to help them with issues of the heart and interpreting their dreams. When the pharaoh of Egypt had a dream that was clearly important but couldn't understand its meaning, he heard of Joseph and called him out of prison to interpret the dream for him. Not only was Joseph able to interpret the dream, He also knew the heart of God well enough to understand what God wanted to do about the bad news of the famine so all would be saved and even prosper through it. The best part of the story is that God cared so much about the people that He positioned one of His sons to be ready to help when they needed it most. He also made sure that when Joseph came to the rescue, he was able to handle the favor and not let it ruin him internally. In fact, by the time he went through all he did, he had grown to the point of being able to forgive and save the very brothers who had betrayed him. God the

---

15 an Andrew Lloyd Webber musical, Genesis 37

Provider was able to use Joseph to display His love for the people by providing in the midst of potential crisis. Here again we see His heart to make Himself known. God could have just stopped the famine, but He preferred to use it to show His care and desire to provide for them—to make Himself known.

Does Joseph's process sound familiar to your own journey? If so, you'll get a lot out of Johnny's last book, The Seven Mountain Mantle: Receiving the Joseph Anointing for Reforming Nations. *In the same way that Joseph received a mantle of seven colors of favor, each of us is also given a responsibility and privilege of favor to impact the seven areas of culture that need the redemption of God's love. We too must go through a process that prepares us to be able to access God's supernatural solutions for the crises of our day so the authority we function in will not harm us or the people God will position us to serve. What more honored assignment could we have than to experience God's provision for ourselves while He uses us to provide for others? We will do this for the sake of His name and fame—as the God who loves to provide the riches of His love for the nations of the earth. How they will rejoice when they see the truth that God enjoys providing for us and through us!*

WHO IS GOD—AS PROVIDER?

God as our Provider is not Santa Claus, content to be visited once a year with our laundry list of needs. Neither is He a gum-ball machine we can put a little something in and get out what we want. Johnny also likes to remind people that God is not like a mafia boss that we need to pay off with an offering so that He won't break our kneecaps. He is much more relational than we can imagine and more generous than the hosts of Extreme Home Makeover. He has literally provided for every possible need we will ever have emotionally, physically, monetarily, and spiritually. But it doesn't stop there—as One who is bigger than time itself, He has gone into our eternity and already prepared for all we will need there too. We see in every area of culture that God provides Himself and His better plans as the cure. He has even provided us with love so we can have love to give back to Him!

The interesting thing about the different faces of God is that you can't typically see them until you need to see them. Would you know His strength if you weren't weak? Or His jealous pursuit of your heart if you weren't prone to wandering from Him? Would you find Him to be faithful as a Provider if you could do it yourself? Most likely you will never fully appreciate this aspect of God as Provider until you really need to see some tangible provision. The only things that keep Him from supplying Himself and His ways are our pride and tendency to settle for our ways.

One of the best examples Jesus gave us as God the Provider was when He was speaking to thousands and it got late enough in the day that the people needed to leave to find food. Jesus told them to all sit and then, with the help of His disciples, miraculously multiplied a little boy's small lunch of fish and bread to feed them all, with leftovers.[16] God seems to love to wait until what feels like the last minute to us, and then extravagantly bless us with more than enough. Jesus also showed us God's enjoyment in letting us participate in distributing what He provides out of the overflow of the little we make available to Him. It was one thing for that crowd to witness such a supernatural event, but a whole other realization to absorb the significance of what that actually meant—the man standing before them was indeed God in the flesh. God as Provider ends up being better than what we thought we needed in the first place.

INVITE HIM IN—AS PROVIDER

When you see God clearly as the One who Provides extravagantly out of the fullness of who He is, you stop looking to others for what they can give you. When you're confident in His ability to take care of you, you aren't jealous when you see others being taken care of. Your heart can celebrate when others receive what they need because you trust what He has for you. When you see the massive storehouse that God draws from on your behalf, you don't live for money or settle for being a taker. You connect to

---

16 Matthew 14, Mark 6, Luke 9

the process of learning to be a steward of what is His and enjoy partnering with His heart to give.

*Continuing on in our understanding of "The Lord's Prayer," we read in the sixth line Jesus' request of our Father, **"Forgive us our debts as we forgive our debtors."** What an absolute mouthful He invited us to digest in this simple request. "Papa, would You wipe away the things I owe others to the same degree I do that for those who owe me something?" As we said, our hearts follow our treasure or money. To whatever and whomever we're in debt, it has our heart. When a debt is forgiven, our heart is restored. I believe Jesus used the language of debt and debtor to connect us to a bigger picture by the practical issue of money. Obviously we want to ask for God's forgiveness and help in getting out of financial debt, but it's so much more.*

Our debt is our obligation. What happens when you free someone from obligation? The same thing that happens when God freed us from obligation to Him. It's just like the familiar quote that says, "If you love something, set it free. If it comes back to you, it was yours. If it doesn't, it never was." Again we're reminded of God's core value for intimacy based on us having the freedom to choose Him. He has set us free to choose Him. As we learn to free others from what we rightfully expect of them, we learn the value of what God offers us—freedom from the burden that we could never repay to God ourselves. As we give away something precious and valuable, it is then that we realize its profound value to us.

Invite God in as Provider. Ask Him to provide for you as you provide for others. Invite Him to free you from the pressure to provide for yourself, while you discover the blessing of providing for others.

CHAPTER NINE

CREATOR: The Color of Glory
THE SOLUTION FOR OUR ARTS & ENTERTAINMENT

Have you ever been in a hospitality or service-based business like a hotel where the employees are wearing pins that say something like "Catch Me at My Best," encouraging customers to fill out survey cards about their performance? In an attempt to promote excellence in service, the management is seeking positive feedback from happy customers about individual employees. To me, that phrase sums up the essence of what the arts and entertainment world is all about—someone being noticed at his or her best and then given an opportunity to use it to entertain others.

Every one of us was born with a unique glory that is all our own. When we find something we are passionate about and do it to the best of our ability—well enough to make others stop and stare—we have a simplified version of the area of culture called arts and entertainment. The possibilities seem limitless. Here are just some ways we have found to do our best and use it for entertaining others: painting, sculpture, music, dance, drama, comedy, TV, reality shows, films and documentaries, theatre, production, directing, computer animation, literature, poetry, songwriting, blogging, photography, fashion, beauty pageants, design, decor, sports, Olympics, recreational sports, video graphics games, culinary arts, party planning, online social communities, YouTube, and more.

This is the aspect of culture that we could technically survive without but is actually the best part of life. It's everything we do for fun, pleasure, recreation, competition, and creative expression. It validates the existence of our soul by giving place for joy and sorrow, laughter and passion, ordinary and adventure, victory and defeat. Arts and entertainment is a microphone to the collective voice of each generation's distinctive sound, look, and achievements.

If God has a refrigerator in Heaven, it's covered with the masterpieces His sons and daughters have produced throughout the history of the earth. If He has a trophy case, it's filled with the accomplishments of a proud Father's children. He loves it when we express love as glory through the endless media of art and the many ways we have found to entertain and compete.

One of my favorite memories from my childhood is the time I discovered I could get my dad's attention and praise by singing and dancing for him. Out on our porch, I twirled and kicked to the song "The Entertainer" by Scott Joplin playing on our cassette player, while my daddy clapped and encouraged me to kick higher—I must have been about 7. I felt like I was seen, and it made me happy to make him happy. I was ruined for anything else. That's when I knew I was made to wow people—as self-serving as that sounds, I know many can relate. You may have discovered a similar feeling as your dad watched you in sports or something else. Of course that vision and understanding of my call to "greatness" has been refined quite a bit since then, but the simplicity of it remains the same. We were created to move the hearts of those that watch us with what we do and who we are. Isn't that what God does to us—moves our hearts with what He does and who He is? And aren't we made in His image?

When we look at a newborn baby or a sunset until it takes our breath away, it's actually the glory of God that has moved our heart by who He is and what He does. When you do what you do and you are who you are to the point that it moves someone else's heart, you have found your glory. One of the definitions for the Hebrew word for glory is weight or impact, as in the kind of impact you make. One of the definitions of the Greek word glory is reputation, as in how we are perceived by others. What comes to mind when people hear your name? That's your glory. Your glory is your reputation and what makes you **you**. *When you've found the best version of yourself, you've found your true glory. We're not talking about a carefully crafted image or facade—the masked version of you. We're talking about the you that God originally thought of when He made you. Many never find it, and those who do usually do so late in life. Sometimes you display your glory and never realize it because you're simply being you. That's the best kind of glory.*

Once you have tasted glory, it seems impossible to ever be content again with a lesser version of yourself. Of course, many people's glory influences an area of culture that isn't meant to entertain. That's legitimate glory as well, but this part of culture of arts and entertainment is ultimately meant to display the **creative** *heart of God. Every nation's unique forms of art and entertainment point to the part of God's heart that is extravagantly fun and creative. When we see art and entertainment done His way, through our individual expressions, we know Him in a new way and are able to see* **His** *glory.*

LOVE DISPLAYED AS GLORY

Yellow is another color of love seen in our Rainbow God. When we are good at entertaining someone with our talent, creation, or expressed ideas, we have found our place of influence in this particular area of culture that seems to be best represented by this color. Yellow reminds us of costly gold, which is used as the highest honor in award ceremonies. Interestingly, humanity has chosen gold for our monetary standard, as well as the entertainment standard for highest quality and excellence. Yellow also makes us think of the sunshine, which is replicated by spotlights that shine on the celebrities we love to celebrate.

Arts and entertainment is the most influential sphere of culture of this age. We are most definitely an entertainment-dominant generation. Teenage pop stars are followed and idolized more than seasoned adults of wisdom and maturity. The top influencers of society are more likely to have come out of the 'hood than out of Harvard.

This is partly because of the generally jaded views this generation has toward the other spheres of society. Generally speaking, this generation seems to collectively resent the structures of government, religion, media, education, economy, and even their own family. In that vacuum, the arts are often just an opportunity to distract ourselves from the pain and frustration of real life.

As the full-colored God is invited into all the structures of society, they will begin to carry the glory they are meant to carry. All of culture, in addition to entertainment, will become more relevant and important to the younger generation. But for now, the world of arts, sports, and other entertainment dominates the stage and captivates the majority of our attention. We can either complain and bellyache about this or just realize that God isn't overly bothered because He's prepared to compete for our children's hearts, even on this platform of life. After all, He's the original Source of all true creativity. Everything else is either a distortion of His creativity or a greatly watered-down version of it.

In all of the arts and ways we are entertained, love is expressed as glory. God displays His love for us in His creation and through the glory of His creativity coming through us as His children. When we see the glory of His creativity, we encounter an aspect of who He is, and it reminds us that He not only exists but that He loved us enough to give us beauty, humor, symmetry, design, and unfolding drama through what we wrongly refer to as Mother Nature. When we experience the glory of creativity through others, we also encounter God as Love.

Think about this: past the obvious moments of being entertained, we are actually watching someone else's glory or a part of the best version of them. The Olympics is a great example. Even if we know little about a particular sport someone is competing in, our attention is easily captivated by watching a man, woman, or team bring the best they have to give after years of intense preparation for that very moment. Drama is felt in the life stories of all they have overcome, and beauty is seen on the faces of the glorious winners. A masterpiece painting is similar. Most are famous and valuable because of the artists' life story and unique way of expressing what they saw, even many years after their death.

So how does seeing God's or someone else's glory register on our hearts as love? Ultimately, all of our hearts are looking for evidence that we are loved. We find a piece of that evidence when we realize we were each given a glory of our own. When we see someone else's glory, it helps us believe that we also just might have a glory too—a version of ourselves that will touch the hearts of others. And even more than that, it gives us hope that our spirit came from the Spirit of God because, like Him, we too have a glory. When we are awe-struck by His glory in creation, it conditions our hearts to believe that part of us is made like Him with the ability to bring awe and inspiration to the world too. This is a big part of our legitimate need for identity that is rooted in nothing less than God, the Creator Himself.

WHO IS GOD—AS CREATOR?

Why do our children in their early years delight in coloring us pictures and making us pretend gourmet meals out of play-dough? Why do they dance, sing, and recite silly jokes fearlessly for parents who take the time to be an attentive audience? Why do they compete in little league as if they were the ones receiving the million-dollar contracts of professional athletes? I (Elizabeth) would say they do it for three reasons: to be seen, to be enjoyed, and to express passion. When we feel seen and enjoyed and are able to express passion, we have found a safe way to experience emotion. Emotion is part of what makes us feel human and alive. When we stop feeling, we start dying inside. Many people's emotions are so shut down that, without even realizing it, they turn to entertainment as the one safe place they have found to experience tears and laughter, passion and anger, fear and peace. Through art and entertainment, we can turn our emotions on and off at the switch of a button, controlling what we're most afraid of.

Why are we so afraid of our emotions? Emotions are the lid to the pain we hide and protect. We subconsciously guard them perhaps because we think *we simply can't handle what lies beneath them. Pain has a way of making you think it's a bottomless pit that you will never escape or survive if you fall into it. Some have lived through so much pain as children that they have believed they could never survive one more bit of it, so they conclude it's better to bury the pain than to sort back through it. Others hide from expressing emotions because no one ever taught them how to handle and channel them in a healthy way, so they are afraid of losing control in front of others.*

Emotions are also intricately intertwined with our glory. We were meant to show our unique glory like a bird is meant to sing. Our glory is fueled by what we feel passionate enough about that we will sacrifice and work to excel at it or find just the right way to express it. For some, the thing that has become their extraordinary talent or glory is the very thing they learned in order to help them survive their childhood. Some of the best comedians, for example, are those who found humor as a way to make it through profound pain and rejection. Emotions are greatly important to the creative process. They must be accessed in order to find your glory and to find God's glory. When you aren't in touch with your own heart, you will also make poor choices in recognizing authentic glory in someone else and end up settling for art and entertainment that is damaging to you.

*If God created our emotions for anything, He created them for us to experience **Him**. He created us with the ability to feel and emote as a way to respond to Him and His love for us—to give us the potential for a meaningful and intimate relationship with Him outside of the bonds of religion. God longs for us to know Him—all of Him. He wants us to know Him as Creator, not to prove some religious argument against evolution but to make us fully alive. Alive to our own hearts and the world around us. Alive to who we are in Him so we might find our true glory. Our creativity, when it's sourced in Him, provokes others' emotions just like God as Creator intentionally designed the beauty and magnificence of His creation to touch our emotions. The fact that we have emotions is validation that God has emotions too. We are made in His image, so we too are creative and emotional.*

Not only has God given us a palette of emotions to draw from, He has also provided endless colors, sounds and rhythms, art mediums and textures, technologies, words and languages, movements, tastes, and smells to experience life and His heart for us through. God could be called a compulsive creative. In the beginning of time as we know it, God created the backdrop for the history of the world. The Bible describes His weeklong creative binge in the book of Genesis. He made mountains of all sizes, shapes and colors. He made trees of every distinction with fruit of every size, color, shape, and flavor. He made animals of every size, shape, color, demeanor, and personality. He made birds of all variety and fish of every imaginable appearance. Once He was pleased with the creative landscape He made, He placed man in the midst of His creative explosion. He then challenged Adam to use his creativity and give every animal a name.

Even Adam himself is proof that God has so much inexhaustible creativity that there has never been a look-alike since the beginning. You can walk around the entire world and meet all the seven billion plus people on the planet and never find your replica. Should anyone ever find another person even similar in appearance, their voice, likes, dislikes, and personality will ultimately reveal that each of us is totally unique, even among twins. We have a God so compulsively creative that He won't even cookie-cutter snowflakes. Every one must look different, even if He were the only one to notice. No two people have the same fingerprints, eyes, DNA, or even voices. Do you think God as Creator is okay with the widespread assumption that He is boring? He doesn't just know about creativity, He's a walking exhibition in creative genius.

THE LIE:
GOD DOESN'T WANT US TO HAVE FUN

Do you think God the Creator is okay with us not having fun? Is He okay with us not being happy? Or having fun and being happy without Him? As we've stated previously, every area of life and culture that leaves God out as the Source hints of our orphan mentality. When we perceive God as distant and uninterested in our fun, in the context of arts and entertainment, we look like a bunch of children who had to sneak out of the house in the middle of the night in order to go have some real fun because our parents are too strict to allow us what we need. I don't use the word "need" lightly. I (Elizabeth) believe we need to have fun and feel happy as much as we need proper nutrition. We wither in every way without it. It literally affects our body, soul, and spirit when we go through life without enough fun—those things that make us feel happy.

I remember being taught as a teenager in the private Christian school I attended that there is a difference between happiness and joy. Joy is something that is lasting and doesn't come and go depending on our circumstances. You can have true joy even when life is hard, when you trust God is working the difficulties out for your good. The religiosity I was exposed to implied that happiness was another issue altogether. It was thought of as shallow and earthly, therefore something to be extremely careful of how we got it. There was no dancing at our proms. I still don't remember what we did besides get all dressed up and stand around in our school gymnasium—so lame and so far from the heart of our Papa who rejoices over us with singing and dancing.[1]

One of my favorite preachers, Bill Johnson of Bethel Church in Redding, Calif., often talks about the fact that God is not in a bad mood. Have you ever thought of God as happy? Why wouldn't He be? He has nothing to fear, and He has set everything into motion in such a way that He will get what He has always wanted—a people who have chosen to allow Him to lavish His love on them as they grow in their understanding of His heart forever. Because God is not held by time like we are, He already knows what is to come and He is rejoicing as He watches and interacts with our journey of discovering the real Him. And the real Him is happy, creative, fun, and not shut down in His emotions. He wants nothing less for us too.

---

1 Zephaniah 3:17 The word for rejoice in this verse means leaping and dancing in a circle in its original translation.

How do we know He wants us to be happy? When we feel happy, certain chemicals and hormones are released in our bodies that are vital for mental and physical health. When we don't have them, we are depressed and our bodies begin to make extra adrenaline until they can't anymore, causing illnesses and extreme fatigue. When our own ability to produce adrenaline wanes, we tend to settle for addictions that provide a steady adrenaline drip. When we aren't happy very often, we take on the weight of life in ways we were never meant to, and we live under stress that produces excess cortisol with resulting weight gain and related diseases. Why would God make our bodies with the need to feel happy if He wasn't okay with it? Of course, like everything good, it can be pushed outside healthy boundaries and ultimately become an extreme pursuit for happiness, resulting in a source of sorrow instead. But He has clearly wired us for happiness.

For the most part, the way arts and entertainment are currently expressed perpetuates the lie that God isn't fun and He certainly doesn't want us to have fun either. That lie is partially true to the extent we use a wrong definition for fun, so it's important to go ahead and clarify what real fun is by looking at what real entertainment is. Remember, we said entertainment is when someone does something so amazing that it causes us to stop and stare or take notice. It's when we have found the best version of ourselves, our glory. The best version of ourselves would obviously have to do with what produces life in us and in the observer, not death. Yes, people will stop and stare at danger, risk, and even death, but the result is fear, and enough fear eventually kills us from the inside out as individuals and as a society. In a similar way, anything we entertain ourselves with that promotes a lifestyle that eventually brings heartache and pain to us or others is not the best version of us, and therefore is not true creative art or entertainment the way God meant it to be. Fun that leaves us short or long term damaged in any way is, in reality, abuse and should not be considered entertainment.

In order to express our true creativity and glory, we must be in tune with our heart's passion and emotions. Nothing stifles emotions and creativity more than religion. It's no wonder that some of our most famous performers left the church to go into entertainment. Because most of what we know as the church is focused on the rules of religion and not on the love of relationship with God and others, we scare away the most creative among us. Someone who is trying to live under the weight of perfectionism and performance in order to be accepted has very little room to discover their passion and glory because they are using up all their energy to fit someone else's version of the best them. Religion is the opposite of freedom—the kind of freedom that produces life and real happiness is the fertile ground of creativity. And the real God, not man's religious ideas of Him, is the only way to be free enough to truly find the real you and the best you.

HOW DOES THIS LIE ABOUT GOD PLAY OUT IN CULTURE?

When we incorrectly perceive that God doesn't want us to have fun and couldn't care less if we experience happiness in life, then we sing, write, create, and jest about things that further our belief that He either doesn't exist or doesn't care about us. Hearts that don't know their God cares about them do what any child does when he doesn't feel loved—they either try to get attention through destructive behavior, subconsciously daring their parents to intervene, or they simply disconnect their heart from the relationship. When we can't have what we value, we tend to protect our heart by no longer valuing that thing. Most parents have experienced both scenarios. You've seen the ones in grocery stores who are struggling to finish their shopping while a toddler screams in a tantrum so as to assure they remain the center of their mother's world. Other parents know the sadness it brings when you realize you have lost your child's heart because at some point it felt too painful to the child to continue to offer it to you.

If it's God's attention we value and need but can't seem to find, then, like the toddler, we create drama and chaos around us until He steps in to rescue us from ourselves and the destruction we've created. Or we disconnect and distance our heart from God so that we don't have to face the disappointment we feel about our wrong perception of His heart toward us. Either way we choose to respond plays out in the art and entertainment outlets we have *created. We sing, dance, and act out our pain and the rebellion it triggers in us, which continues promoting a false fantasy to the next generation. Generally speaking, with rare exceptions, celebrities end up promoting a destructive lifestyle as normal, healthy fun, when in reality it's born out of rejection and disappointment with God. That doesn't make their performances or life work inherently evil, but it's destructive in that what they do, say, or sing about lulls others into the false conclusions of their own broken hearts. They were given genuine gifts from God to express creativity and excellence through, but they found only a portion of their glory—their best broken self rather than their best healed self.*

Like every other area of culture, this cycle continues to advance a lie about what God is really like. The next generation buys it, repackages it, and sells it again. When those who are in the arts and entertainment industry find the personal glory that God gave them coming from of a healed perspective of God, they will feel validated and seen by Him as His son or daughter who is able to be enjoyed and delighted in. It will overflow into whatever their particular expression is and into their personal lifestyle as a celebrity, and it will help break the cycle we have become stuck in. They will create and compete in ways that cause us to believe God is near and He is good. It's not that their life's work won't be true to life and authentic, but the conclusions they lead us to will be life giving.

THE TRUTH:
GOD WANTS US TO ENJOY LIFE!

To enjoy means to find pleasure in. God as Creator wants us to find pleasure in the midst of everyday life. Creativity that reflects Him and is a response to His love will provoke emotions in the observer that eventually lead to pleasure—something that pleases in the truest sense. Jesus said that the truth will set you free.[2] When what we celebrate through art and entertainment is founded in the truth of who God is and how involved He is in our lives, then this area of culture will create freedom in the hearts of the ones

---

2   John 8:32

being entertained. Freedom. Not addictions or bondage to perversions that leave us forever unsatisfied. Jesus described Satan as a thief who comes only to steal, kill, and destroy. Unfortunately we often partner with this enemy without realizing it and become instruments of pillage, death, and destruction ourselves through the very area we were meant to display love and life by discovering our personal glory. Jesus went on to say that He came to give us life abundantly.[3] That means fullness of life to such a degree that it goes beyond what we need or require. It is extravagant living that He offers us. Who doesn't want that?!

Jesus wasn't talking about some "hide from the scary world because it might taint us" kind of living. Nor did He live that way Himself. If I (Elizabeth) could apologize as a Christian to the entertainment industry, I would. I would say how sorry I am that we have pointed fingers of judgment while we offered no solutions ourselves and refused to bless and make room for the creativity God wanted to pour through you because it looked different than the boxes we made for you. A lot of what comes out of Hollywood is indeed toxic, but a lot is truly amazing and inspiring. The enemy of God loves it when we accuse one another and miss out on each other's strengths, furthering his destructive patterns in our lives—our bondage to religion and Hollywood's bondage to perversion. It's all the same in the eyes of the One who made us all to be free. God wants us free from religion and free from perversion. Whatever someone is in bondage to produces the same result—art and entertainment that is absent of light. Nothing thrives the way it was meant to apart from light. I am sad for Christians' part in that.

In understanding God's love for art and entertainment and the ways He wants to make life fun for us, we must ask and answer the question, "What is true creativity?" True creativity is a release from God the Creator's heart that lifts our spirits. True creativity has no other source. Apart from Him we have zero creativity. To the degree that we separate from God as Creator, we have no ability to even think creatively—in the true sense of what creativity is.

---

3 John 10:10

Those who choose to be distant from God in Hollywood and the music industry, and even in the church, can only come up with a distorted version of creativity. That is it. They are unable to create anything original and can only copy, counterfeit, or repackage existing creative expressions. We have so dumbed down our definition of creativity that false reproductions are labeled as creative originals. God creates. Satan distorts and counterfeits. We can choose our source of inspiration, from God or Satan, but we are never neutral even when we think we are. This is true in every area of society.

True creativity lifts the soul. False creativity drags the soul down. Hollywood's supposed creative genius is seen in two primary functions: sex and death. All fashion, songs, and movies produced from those who wrongly perceive God will either pander to lust or death and self-destructive themes. Dark and sexually charged themes are not creative—they are simply distortions of something that was good in its pure state. Sex is one of our greatest gifts from God, but only remains so when His accompanying guidelines are followed. It is always ultimately counterproductive and disaster-laden when we connect sexually with someone outside of the parameters of a covenant marriage relationship between a man and a woman.

We somehow can't seem to accept this guideline. Everything else in life comes with rules and restrictions, but we somehow want sex with no rules. For example, basketball is a great sport, but it isn't just about being able to dribble the ball and shoot. You must be able to function within the rules of the game if you want to play. You can't just start when you want to start or pile on five extra people on your side when you're losing. You can't walk with the ball without dribbling or run people over while getting the ball. You can't play while the clock is off. There are parameters to the game. All sports are meant to be played in the context of the rules accompanying that sport. Nobody cares to even watch sports that are played without rules.

The same is true for where and how you work. You work where you are told, when you are told, by the rules of that workplace. Even if you are an entrepreneur, you have to create your own guidelines for work or you'll end up acting as a bum. You also can't build a house without codes, inspections, and limitations. The home can't be constructed too close to the curb or too high, nor can it be painted a tacky color.

All of life tells us that every good thing that exists functions within the context of rules and limitations. The rules for our sexuality are given by the One who created us as sexual beings, and we simply must start heeding those rules or we'll continue to suffer the severe consequences in our lives and culture. Immorality is everything that falls outside of God's set of rules for how sex will remain a blessing to us. All sexual activity outside the bounds established by God puts us in Satan's territory of stealing, killing, and destroying. He allows us to ascend a grand cliff through addictions and sexual promiscuity that allures us with false freedom to do as we please, only to be later thrown off to our death from its highest peak. God figured out how this great gift of sex would work to our best and gave us the clear context of marriage for it. All other sexual fulfillment and intercourse will result in some level of our separation from God who was the One who created it for us to begin with. How dumb is that?

Once we have decided to ignore the "manufacturer's guidelines," we're disconnected from God being what we need Him to be in our lives. All areas of entertainment look like a virtual battlefield of casualties and walking wounded because so many entertainers refuse God's better ways for us.

God doesn't just tolerate sports, music, fashion, dance, and movies; He actually loves them. He gave us the concepts behind all of them. I believe they all exist in heaven. In heaven everything functions according to God's better ways of doing things. I assume that no one there desires to do things differently because there is such a glory to true creativity, and with it comes the real freedom we are so desiring. I believe in Heaven we'll see some of the most inspiring movies imaginable played on much more advanced technology than we have dreamed of. Surely all of our senses and emotions will be impacted to the max, and we'll be inspired beyond belief. That kind of creativity is available now for those who recognize that they are sons and daughters of God the Creator. If you will draw near to Him as your Source for creativity, He would love to download to you stories, songs, and talent that will rock this world. He will pour glory through you. He delights in seeing us find our glory, our best version of us. The download process comes out of relationship and intimacy with Him. It comes from choosing to live for Him, with Him, and through Him. It comes through knowing Him as Creator.

HOW CAN WE COOPERATE WITH GOD AS CREATOR IN RESTORING GLORY TO ARTS & ENTERTAINMENT?

In heaven, there are songs, lyrics, movies, books, dances, and expressions of art that we have never thought of or heard, and they are waiting to be released on earth. There are sounds that would make us feel like we were being positively raptured. These new creations are also "available for download." "On earth as it is in heaven" is still the working theme. Satan can't compete with this music. His dissonant sounds that masquerade as creativity are no match for the real. Twisted sounds and lyrics only seem creative when compared to the "same ole, same ole." Just because someone is driven to be compulsively different doesn't mean they have tapped into their authentic glory. Many pop stars have found ways to set new trends with bizarre fashion statements and behavior, but weird shouldn't be confused with God-inspired creativity.

The real question that will clarify if we are helping restore true glory to arts and entertainment is this: What are we promoting to the hearts of those we are entertaining through what we have created? If you are a celebrity or hope to be one, you must ask yourself if you are displaying the light of God and His heart of love and true freedom, or are you promoting bondage to perversion, addictions, and darkness? Truly there is no neutral ground. I (Elizabeth) am not at all saying that what you create must be directly about God, but if your passion is for art, entertainment, or sports, you carry great responsibility and accountability for what you promote in all you do and in your lifestyle. The world is literally watching as you perform for an audience of One. There are many great role models for what we are talking about, like Bono, Tyler Perry, and Tim Tebow, to name a few. As far as I am aware of, they do not compromise the truth of the God they have come to know while they are releasing their unique expression of glory for our entertainment. They take their position seriously in terms of lifestyle, authenticity, relationships, service, and excellence. And in the end, if you look for it you can find evidence that they give God their genuine gratitude and worship for what He does through them.

The world of sports has been in crisis in recent years because of the proliferation of cheating through illegal drugs, steroids, and "potions." These scandals have stolen the glory of sports as the greatest heroes have been found to be operating outside the rules. There's that dirty word again—rules. Steroids are ethically wrong because they change the level playing field. Athletes are rewarded not for the stewardship of their gift, but by covertly breaking the rules. Steroids are also part of Satan's "get rich quick" scheme. This enemy offers a shortcut to stardom and then throws you down from the top. Barry Bonds, Mark McGwire, and Roger Clemens are just a few of the many names of those who have gone to the top and then been thrown down. Satan always seduces us to go outside the rules. You cannot co-labor with God the Creator in sports if you are in violation of the rules. You co-labor with Him not by just calling yourself a Christian but by actually doing things His way—the right way.

The glory of an athlete is that he or she has persevered with an athletic gift to such a degree that their craft stirs the hearts of the spectators to want to celebrate with them. Success in sports gives them a platform to redirect the glory back to God the Creator. All attention that comes to us is meant to be redirected back to the Creator. Hollywood seems to instinctively know that, and you often hear God acknowledged at award ceremonies even by those that otherwise don't appear to have a real relationship with Him. The problem is that most of what celebrities are honored for involved their promoting those things that keep us from true freedom. Not all, but most. Still, the instinct is there because all creative people know that He is their source for whatever creativity they actually carry.

If what you do "creatively" erodes societal moral fabric, then it truly is the counterfeit. If what you do serves to lift our spirits by pointing us to the truth about who God really is, then what you have is real creativity and the genuine glory you were made to live from. You are then co-laboring with God the Creator and are a minister with a platform and pulpit that is more powerful and influential than those found in most churches.

THERE IS ONE ENEMY
IN THE WAR OVER ARTS & ENTERTAINMENT

There is one enemy in this great spiritual war that's taking place over arts and entertainment, and specifically over Hollywood. Satan shows up in this industry much like the biblical woman Jezebel, so we will refer to him as Jezebel in this area of culture.[4] More than anyone, Satan understands the amazing glory and grandeur of true creativity. As Jezebel, he knows God's love for creating and loves to poison it through deceiving the sons and daughters of God by either using them to spew his filth or run and hide from it, therefore robbing from it the light it was meant to promote.

4 Jezebel was a queen of Israel's northern kingdom and also a priestess of the false god Baal. She was highly manipulative and insistent in establishing Baal-worship as the national religion. Figuratively, she was used in Revelation 2 as a symbol of seducing people away from the true worship of God. 1 Kings 16:31; 18:3-4,19 19:1-2; 21-25; 2 Kings 9:30-37; Revelation 2:20-23

I (Johnny) have been told by producers in Hollywood that they are in a creativity crisis. They are having a more difficult time than ever finding fresh, new scripts and story lines that will amaze the masses. Why? The obvious answer is that God the Creator is not being invited in. Jezebel has enthroned herself by offering "get rich quick" schemes in Hollywood, and it has sapped the creativity even out of some of the most creative people. When you sell your soul and yield to Jezebel, she will make a deal with you that most can't refuse. She promises wealth and stardom, but at the expense of true creativity that brings life instead of death, and ultimately at the expense of one's soul. As has happened in the sports world, Jezebel will take you to the top of the entertainment mountain, use you to promote her cycle of celebrating all that is shallow and dark, and then throw you off as she has done with star after star.

The following is a short list of recognizable names that Jezebel has tragically, in some way or another, prematurely taken their lives. Sadly, each were connected to at least one ingredient of her triple-seduction cocktail of drugs, alcohol, and suicide. Whitney Houston, Don Cornelius, John Belushi, Marilyn Monroe, Richard Burton, Kurt Cobain, Chris Farley, Judy Garland, Jimi Hendrix, Michael Jackson, Janis Joplin, Heath Ledger, Anna Nicole Smith, River Phoenix, Elvis Presley, Freddie Prinze, and Amy Winehouse are among the many.

All of these made it to the top but were eventually thrown down by Jezebel. She gave them the stardom they wanted and then did her typical stealing, killing, and destroying she loves to do, no matter what kind of relationship they may or may not have had with God. (I'm not saying none of these people were in a relationship with God, but they were still victims of Satan's influence.) This list is only some with highly recognizable names, but tragically it actually runs in the hundreds and probably thousands when you include the porn and fashion industry suicides and drug-related deaths.

THE HOPEFUL FUTURE FOR ARTS & ENTERTAINMENT

There's always good news, even for structures that are presently under a good bit of darkness. The first good news is that light will always ultimately prevail over darkness. God the Creator will defeat Satan and his Jezebel ways through His awakened sons and daughters who will know and love Him as the Source for true creativity. They will find their glory and learn to arise and shine with His glory.[5] They will not be afraid of competing with the present standards and loving those who are stuck in compromise and the lesser versions of their personal glory.

Jezebel will be crushed on the very mountain she has cast these sons and daughters from, but not simply by fasting and prayer meetings of the righteous or by hiding from the overall industry. Jezebel will be crushed by the coming tsunami of God's children who will see and know Him in His goodness and light and then re-image Him in all of society. This army of rising sons and daughters will so connect to the Creator that there will be no room left for Jezebel or any desire for her lesser offers. It will become apparent to all that the best music, stories, directing, and creativity of every sort is coming from those who have authentic relationships with God. She will lose her power to entice and addict the ones filled with God's talent and gifts.

The new levels of creativity and success will manifest not through those who sold their souls to make it big but through those who enjoy life from a position of true freedom and have learned to co-labor with God the Creator. They will not be motivated by money and fame but will indeed make great sums of money and carry fame that doesn't change them or push them to compromise. Their chief concern will be God's fame and the privilege of doing their part to love and uplift society by displaying His love and glory. A great uplifting of society will come out of what God begins to release even

---

5   Isaiah 60:1-3

from Hollywood. I (Johnny) believe that in time, for a season, it will even be known as "Holy-wood" because of the great thing God will do among those who love to create.

I believe there will be new fashions downloaded from heaven. These fashions will carry the light and glory of our Creator, and masses will want to wear them. Those who co-labor with God the Creator will download new dance steps and moves, as well as new sports and techniques, from heaven. Those who know the real God will access from Heaven amazing art that will even "oooh" and "aaah" atheists. Simply said, the best of days are ahead for true lovers of creativity. God is not challenged in the least by what is presently being marketed in our art and entertainment world. He's just looking for His kids to know this and invite Him in as Creator. It's really going to be fun to watch the changes come.

When arts and entertainment are done God's better way, casualties will not continue to be strewn across our celebrity headlines. Those who have the privilege of affecting the masses through creativity will steward well over their influence, using it to promote directly or indirectly the true heart of God for the world. They will use the truth they have discovered about God's goodness and power to overcome every lie, to teach the next generation how to live authentic lives with God in the center of relationships in a real and non-religious way. Many currently in the industry will have radical conversion experiences with God and will no longer be ashamed to go to Him as their Source. They will extravagantly use their wealth to bring creative solutions to the worst problems on the globe and want no credit for it. They will weep at award ceremonies because of the presence of God as Creator among them. Are you ready?!

INVITE HIM IN—AS CREATOR

*Jesus' prayer that began with "Our Father" ends with **"lead us not into temptation, but deliver us from evil, for Yours is the kingdom and the power and the glory forever, amen."** Jesus was teaching us the basics of* *how to talk with our Papa. This last part of "The Lord's Prayer" has always surprised me (Elizabeth). Why would we need to request that God not lead us to moments in our lives where we are tempted, but rather deliver or rescue us? Wouldn't a good God already know we need that? Yes, but sometimes what we ask for is more about aligning our hearts with truth than about needing to persuade Him of something.*

Temptation is the testing of our integrity. Integrity is when what is on the inside and outside of us matches. It's when who we are in our core is the same as who we show others. This is something those in entertainment are particularly lacking. Celebrities become masters at giving their fans the image that impresses and sells while they waste away behind closed doors. But there's a way out. By praying this request like Jesus did, we are acknowledging that there's a test of evil compromise and we know that, left to ourselves, we're unable to pass it. We're acknowledging our need to be rescued by our Papa from evil.

Many don't even believe that evil exists or understand their relationship to it. Evil is real in every sense—as Satan, who is after us as the object of God's love and affection and as anything that brings us pain and hardship. In our relationships with God, we must learn to dialogue with Him about the reality of our weakness when it comes to evil. We are not evil, and we are not the enemy. Each of us, as we connect to God through what Jesus did for us on the cross, is a son or daughter of this amazing Father who delights in coming to our rescue when we invite Him to. Do you need His creative solutions to get you out of the grip of temptation and evil? Just invite Him in as Creator. Not only will He use His creativity to extricate you from what holds you back, but He will also awaken His creativity and the unique glory you were born to have.

Perhaps you're entrenched so deeply in the quicksand of compromise that you honestly don't see any way out. Even if you did, you feel too weak to know how to ask. All it takes is a look His way and a genuine cry for help. You will see that He is strong enough to cover for your weakness and His compassion is greater than your shame. All you've ever wanted and needed is in His arms, so run into Him. If you really want Him to, He will teach you how to feed your spirit with the truth of who He is instead of the filth you've been settling for. He understands that you reacted to the lies about Him and the disappointments of life and landed in compromise, addictions, and perversions you never thought you would. He also understands the way out, if you're willing to follow His lead. Especially if you're in this industry, if you will humble yourself and admit that you have compromised and been used to promote compromise to others, then you'll begin a powerful process of personal redemption that will most definitely spill over into your creative works.

The entertainment industry that was meant to give us the happiness and reprieve from the monotony and difficulties of life is a poor substitute for what you can find simply by sitting alone with Him and feasting on His love and presence. It isn't as instant as turning on the TV or your laptop, but it is worth learning how to wait for as you prioritize just sitting still with Him and doing nothing else. The industry will one day be a reflection of that love and life-giving presence you find in Him, but it will still pale in comparison to the glory that is Him. If you really want to be free, you must learn to grow strong from the inside out. Determine to find ways to feed your spirit until you carry the light of Jesus in you.

*God as Creator dispels darkness by creating light. He doesn't run from darkness or evil by taking a stand against it. He simply shows up and it leaves. He shows up with the love that is in His glory (what makes Him **Him**) and His creativity. God shows up through His boys and girls who have found their own glory, overflowing love, and radical creativity. God wants to show up through your glory and His light in you.*

Jesus ends the infamous Lord's Prayer by teaching us to always remember and declare from our hearts that God's kingdom (His better way of doing everything), God's power (His ability to accomplish things), and God's glory (His correct reputation) is what this experience on earth is ultimately all about. He is big enough and good enough not to need us, but kind and relational enough to want us in on all He's doing. His love rescues you and then leaves you with limitless ways to show others the love He poured out to you.

CHAPTER TEN

What Does <u>Love</u> Look Like Coming Out of <u>You</u>?

*You were made for love. God intended from the beginning to teach us how to be loved and how to love. We were never meant to try to earn it, muster it up on our own, or clamor our way through life looking for it. It has been here—**He** has been here—all along. You may have spent your whole life feeling distant from God, only to find that you were closer than you thought—just not the part of Him that anyone told you was Him. As you have expanded your perspective of who God is as the God of all of life, are you beginning to see that He is the passion you were born with? He is the thing you love and value the most about life. Maybe you just never knew it was Him because it never felt like it matched your version or someone else's version of God.*

*But now you know! You've been loved with extravagant measure from a God who is Love. He defines Love, and He **is** Love. And He chose you to come alive to the reality of Him in this time in history, in this generation, all so He could make you the recipient of this great Love of His. So what are you going to do about it? Where will you spend this love—on whom and on what?*

First, will you let it in? Will you invite Love into every corner of your heart and every cell of your body, beyond any walls you've constructed to

213

protect yourself, and beyond your ability to understand it? Will you allow Love to wake you up on the inside so you can feel Him and know Him the way you were originally created to? Put the book down for a minute and just be loved. Ask God to let you know His love in a fresh way that you never have before. We hesitate to do things like this often because we're afraid in our heart of hearts that we will be disappointed—that He won't show up for us like we think He does for others. Listen, you can trust that whatever He does, whether it's some supernatural encounter or a quiet knowing in your core, He is real, and His love is real. He will blow into your spirit like He first did with Adam and Eve because that's the kind of God He is. He is not distant. He breathed life into them face to face and mouth to mouth to quicken their bodies to life with the essence of His own Spirit.[1] He still does that today for those hungry enough to ask Him for it.

Just because at times we don't feel like He loves us doesn't make it any less true. So much of even this natural world, like gravity for instance, is proof that what we cannot see is still quite real. His love is real. He lavishes love on us so we have more than enough to love Him well with, love our-selves well with, and love others with. He's a good Papa in that He provides for us the very thing He longs for from us. He has set us up to succeed in every way that matters for eternity and the big picture. But we have to continue to go to Him for that love that we so desperately need and not keep settling for the counterfeit, lesser things, and quick fixes. When we go anywhere else for it, we'll come up eventually profoundly empty every time.

God sent Jesus to heal our perspective of God, to sacrifice Himself for the sin that comes between us and Him, and to make intimacy with our God an option for us. In the most simple way to say it— He wants to be close to us and He did what was needed for the distance to be erased. Anything that tells you that He or His love is distant is a lie. Whatever area of your life and heart that feels distant from God needs His love. Whatever you feel distant from needs to be healed simply by asking Him to do it. Do you feel distant from Him? From your own heart and emotions? From your purpose

---

1   Genesis 2:7

and identity? From your true self and the best version of you—your glory? Do you feel distant from the family and friends you really wish you could love the way you know you were meant to? Stay connected to Him, to Love, and watch the distance evaporate. It's His specialty!

True Love cannot be quenched, cannot fade, cannot run out, and only increases in every way. True Love set time, space, and eternity into motion. True Love imagined you into existence and sustains you to this moment. When True Love is recognized, it's irresistible. Your life's job description is this: to learn to be loved by God with this True Love, no matter what things look like on the outside, so that True Love comes through you to others in your areas of passion and influence. Learn what True Love looks like coming out of you.

THE LIE:
YOUR LIFE DOESN'T REALLY MATTER

What is it that makes us want to find significance in life? If we're supposedly just some life form that evolved and will stop existing when our body dies, then why does our need to feel loved, valued, and wanted seem to be wired into us from before our first breath? Why are we so connected to our hopes and dreams, fears and failures, and desires for more than we can see? It makes sense that the One who created us with our various capacities to navigate all of those thoughts put those in us because they are meant to lead us to the answers, to the Source, to Truth, to Him. It all started in Him, and it will all end in Him. But with Him, the end is actually the beginning.

What we are going after here is the poison that every one of us has been tempted to swallow—that my life doesn't really matter. The fact that we can think and feel that way means an answer to that longing exists. And the resounding truth is that each of us is much more significant than we hope we are, no matter what we are like. What gives us this significance? How do we know we are indeed important?

First of all, if you haven't noticed yet, there's quite a bit of wrestling going on around you and in you. That gunfire you have grown accustomed to hearing just above your head is all about you and your search for significance. Someone knows that if you discover who you really are and how much you really matter, you'll be unstoppable in your pursuit of knowing God, your real Father. That same someone really doesn't want the real God to be known. If you don't matter so much, then why were you born on the front lines of a war zone?

Also, if you remember back when we talked about our value, we said that Jesus' death and all that He sacrificed for us is the proof of our value and worth. Because we are so very valuable to our Papa, He sent Jesus to redeem us. So many who have settled for religion over relationship have wrongly thought that it is only God **in** *us that makes us valuable. No, He created you and declared your value apart from Himself. Because He values you, He gave you the opportunity to choose intimacy with Him. He gives us that choice every day. When we really get that, we not only settle the issue of our worth in our own hearts, we also begin to properly value each other, no matter what our differences may be. This may sound too simplistic, but as far as I (Elizabeth) am concerned, we're all just children of God who have varying levels of the realization of that fact.[2]*

Finally, life in itself is precious, and therefore as long as we have life, we matter. The good news is, if you choose to connect to the Source of all life, then even when your body fails and dies, your spirit will continue to live forever, and you will be given a new body that cannot ever die.[3] Because we have believed the lie that we don't matter, we have not only not valued ourselves, but we greatly undervalue all life. When the culture around us has degraded to such a place that life is not considered as precious in all forms and at all stages, we will always struggle to believe our personal worth. What permeates the culture permeates our soul, individually and collectively.

---

2   Of course we all, as sons and daughters of God, must relate to Him through Jesus Christ and the sacrifice He made on the cross in order to be saved eternally from the effects of sin. John 1:12, Romans 8:14-17, Galatians 4:4-7
3   1 Corinthians 15:35-57

HOW DOES THIS LIE ABOUT YOU
PLAY OUT IN YOUR LIFE?

When you don't believe that you matter, you treat yourself, others, and God like they don't matter so much either. Life feels pointless so you either live without purpose or you make one up and have to work hard to not let it fall apart. When you have no purpose, you wander and react rather than focus, follow through, and respond. You're unlikely to be proactive in what is most important and will major on either escaping reality as often as possible and/or focus on taking care of yourself because of a profound sense of loneliness. You feel that the weight of your whole life is on you because you subconsciously believe God won't protect and take care of you if you don't do it yourself. Basically, you live exhausted internally because it takes a whole lot of energy to survive alone. But don't be fooled, a lack of significance doesn't mean you haven't found some version of a successful life. The real test is internal, not external.

When you feel insignificant, you're like that cartoon character that is so hungry that every animal it looks at appears to him as a tasty meal. When you're starving for the significance you actually already have, you may not mean to, but you look at others mostly for what they can give you. For some, their neediness spills out as abuse or just plain old meanness, addictions, workaholism, or a tendency to be emotionally complicated or emotionally shut down. Now that I have described all of us, you shouldn't feel lonely anymore!

THERE IS ONE ENEMY IN THE WAR
OVER <u>YOUR</u> SIGNIFICANCE

This war always has been and will always be about intimacy with God. The ammo that is used against us and God will always be lies. Some good news is that we are on the same side God is on, although that's what makes us a target. But it also means that the war is actually His to fight as we hide ourselves in the reality of Him and the truth about who we are to Him. We are learning to contend for the truth in our own hearts about who we are and who God is. These cannot be separated because we're made in His image and by Him, and therefore the truth about who we are can only be found in the truth of who He is.

Once we learn the truth of who He is and then the truth of who He says we are, we learn to contend for that truth that we've found about Him to be seen in culture as well. What we gain on a personal level we can give away and communicate in the bigger scope of life and the areas of culture that we're involved in. In both contexts, we are ultimately contending for the knowledge of and intimacy with the real God.

Our battle is certainly not with people. Nor is this some strategy to take over the world. It's a battle over darkness and any lie that has been propagated about how good the God of Love is. Darkness and lies are sourced not in people but in Satan and the demonic realm that follows him. If Christians understand anything, let it be this: If God values intimacy enough with us to give us the freedom to choose it or not (evidenced by the fact that He could easily reveal Himself in such a way that there is utterly no choice), then how much more should we protect everyone's freedom across this globe to choose Him or not? That same freedom gives us the right to love others no matter what choice they make as we offer them a new perspective of this Papa who loves without limits.

We simply must settle, once and for all, the two most important truths for all children of God. Number one, He is good no matter what life's circumstances tempt you to believe about Him. And number two, you are very important. *How do we settle these two issues in our hearts? How do we contend for the truth of who the real God is?*

War and win with your words. We mentioned this before, but it must be said again. You can think the right thoughts all day long, but until your brain hears your voice speak the truth, it won't create a new pathway of thought or a new option of response to whatever you go through. You can read this book all the way through, have believed what you read is true, and understood the lies you have believed about God and yourself. But if you don't create an ongoing new way of thinking, you'll continue to live and react out of the lies you believed.

At the end of this chapter, you will find a code that you can use to access a helpful list of Truth Statements on our website, www.RainbowGod.com. We encourage you to download and print them from the website so that you can read them out loud to yourself every day. Deal a final blow to the thoughts that torment you and undermine your intimacy with God and who He created you to be. Because the truth is, you are worth it. Even though I have had a strong relationship with God my entire life, it wasn't until a few years ago when I began to speak truth out loud to myself daily, that I began to live from a place of true confidence in God. Things drastically changed for me in every way—spiritually, emotionally, and even my health is better than it's ever been!

WHO ARE <u>YOU</u>—AS <u>HIS</u>?

*In each chapter we've looked into an aspect of who God is—as Papa, as Redeemer, as King, as Communicator, as Teacher, as Provider, and as Creator. One of the things I love about God is what Johnny calls the divine humility of God. Johnny will often preach about how, in God's humility, each part of the Trinity is always pointing to the other. Jesus points us to our Father, and our Father sent us Jesus, and Jesus sent us the Holy Spirit, who is always revealing the Father and Jesus to us. In a similar way, God's divine humility is seen when we look to Him. As we learn to see Him correctly, we can't help but realize it's all about Him. But when we finally get that and express that we want to live for Him, we realize He's looking back into our hearts and expressing that **He** is all about **us**!*

We have expanded our view of Him, and now He wants us to expand our view of ourselves. He wants us to discover our value and purpose and live lives that are full of Him and the adventure He planned for us in making the real Him known. Another question to explore becomes who are YOU—as HIS?

*You are not an orphan who was abandoned and rejected by your **Papa**. Because of your great value, you don't need to work hard and be good in order to know God. You have a **Redeemer**, Jesus Christ, who gave His life so that you could be intimate with Him. This **King** cares about you and, in fact, you are royalty. God is constantly a **Communicator**, communicating with you His good plans for you and is patiently teaching the ears of your heart to hear Him. He is your personal **Teacher** and loves that you are completely dependent on Him. As a good **Provider**, He is your Source and delights in providing for you and through you to others. Your **Creator** has given you your own unique glory and wants you to enjoy life. You were made in His image, so who you are is as vast and as amazing as He is. Even as I write this, my own heart has a hard time believing that, but it's true.*

Who am I? I am His. I belong to Him. I live for Him and in Him. I am written in His heart, and He is written in mine. As I search out His heart, I will find mine.

THE TRUTH:
<u>YOU</u> HAVE IMPORTANT THINGS TO DO AND SAY

If the lie is about your lack of significance, then the truth is about your great worth. Because you are valuable to God, He has given you an equally valuable assignment. He has trusted us with His very reputation and prepared a grand treasure hunt so that we can enjoy the journey of discovering the real Him. As we discover the truth and quickly give it away, it leads to more truth. The more we shine, the more light invades our path, our culture, and our world. The more light, the less darkness. So how exactly do we shine? The same way the rainbow does on a rainy day.

You can see a rainbow whenever the Sun shines from behind you and you are looking into water droplets ahead of you suspended in the atmosphere. As the rays of white light hit the drops of water, the light rays bend in each tiny droplet just enough to refract and reflect back to those observing as seven distinct colors. The colors were there all along in the light streaming from the Sun, but we can't see them until they come through in the rain.

In the same way, our Rainbow God can appear distant and colorless until we learn to see Him as He really is coming through each other and the difficulties we go through. The tears and sweat from life's hardships end up becoming the best opportunity to see His goodness displayed as the seven colors of love.

Reflect the light that you see in Him. Be the best version of you and allow the Light of who He is to pass through you. Because you choose to know the real Him, those who look into the storms of life can see the kind of God that He really is as Rainbow God—the God who truly does care about every nation, every area of culture, and each life. There is nothing more important that you could do or say with your life. You have important things to do, so do them with all of your might. You have important things to say, so say them with your whole heart until the knowledge of the glory of God covers the world and all have had the opportunity to choose Him in all His beautiful colors of love.

HOW CAN YOU COOPERATE WITH GOD IN RESTORING CULTURE THAT REFLECTS HIS LOVE?

One day when Jesus was teaching, He explained what the end of time will be like:

"When the Son of Man comes in His glory, and all the holy angels with Him, then He will sit on the throne of His glory. All the nations will be gathered before Him, and He will separate them one from another, as a shepherd divides his sheep from the goats. And He will set the sheep on His right hand, but the goats on the left. Then the King will say to those on His right hand, 'Come, you blessed of My Father, inherit the kingdom prepared for you from the foundation of the world: for I was hungry and you gave Me food; I was thirsty and you gave Me drink; I was a stranger and you took Me in; I was naked and you clothed Me; I was sick and you visited Me; I was in prison and you came to Me.'

"Then the righteous will answer Him, saying, 'Lord, when did we see You hungry and feed You, or thirsty and give You drink? When did we see You a stranger and take You in, or naked and clothe You? Or when did we see You sick, or in prison, and come to You?' And the King will answer and say to them, 'Assuredly, I say to you, inasmuch as you did it to one of the least of these My brethren, you did it to Me.'

"Then He will also say to those on the left hand, 'Depart from Me, you cursed, into the everlasting fire prepared for the devil and his angels: for I was hungry and you gave Me no food; I was thirsty and you gave Me no drink; I was a stranger and you did not take Me in, naked and you did not clothe Me, sick and in prison and you did not visit Me.'

"Then they also will answer Him, saying, 'Lord, when did we see You hungry or thirsty or a stranger or naked or sick or in prison, and did not minister to You?' Then He will answer them, saying, 'Assuredly, I say to you, inasmuch as you did not do it to one of the least of these, you did not do it to Me.' And these will go away into everlasting punishment, but the righteous into eternal life." [4]

A couple of years ago, we toured the historic U.S. penitentiary on Alcatraz Island in San Francisco Bay that housed some of America's most dangerous criminals from the 1930's to '60's. It was so sad to be in that prison for obvious reasons, but this prison is particularly oppressive because of how removed it is from civilization as a literal island. At the time, I had been thinking quite a bit about the words of Jesus you just read and was reminded of what He said about being in prison. As I walked the rows of tiny cells, I imagined how profoundly lonely and worthless each man must have felt as he sat in his cell year after year without having anyone visit him. Talk about believing the lie that you don't matter! For those of us who have never been in

---

4   Matthew 25:31-46

prison, it's probably impossible for us to fathom the significance of even one person making the effort to visit us. But surely if we were there and someone visited us, it would say this one thing to our heart—that we matter and are cared about.

After pondering this description from Jesus of the account all nations and people will give one day of the choices we have made, I believe there are several relevant points He is communicating to us that will serve as a final way of expanding our perspective of God. Notice He does not divide us according to the many things we could list as good and bad in our eyes. Consider how He chooses to explain the whole wrap-up of the end of time as a sorting of nations and people according to one basic idea. Did we recognize Him even in the least and lowliest among us, and did we care about what and who He cares about enough to let them know their worth to Him?

Some have taken these Bible verses to mean that God really wants us to be kind to the ones He highlights here by taking care of the poor, hungry, thirsty, strangers, sick, and prisoners. Of course that is understood, but if you notice, He didn't separate us based on the solutions we brought to them. If so, certainly He would have instructed us to teach the hungry to grow food and to dig wells for the thirsty. He would have told us to help the strangers and those who need clothes to find jobs so they can afford clothing and homes, lead prisoners to Christ, and heal the sick. Obviously those are also important things for us to do and the Bible reiterates that in other ways.

*I believe that Jesus was giving us a clue about who God is. He isn't simply One who wants us to care for the needy, as important as that is. When He says we did it to **Him** when we did it to the least of these, He is telling us an important reality about **Himself**. He equates Himself with the most needy among us. Each needy person Jesus spoke of has this in common—they are in a life circumstance that would make it nearly impossible to believe that anyone cares about them or that they matter. When you are at the bottom of life without the most basic needs of food, water, shelter, and clothing and you are so sick or stuck in prison that you are utterly alone, you most likely end up in the worst crisis of all—the belief that God doesn't exist or that He doesn't see you. When you don't feel like you have even one person who cares about* *you and reaches out to you in some tangible way, it's practically impossible to believe that God cares about you. The greatest desire of God's heart is that each of His children have the opportunity to know that He loves them, cares about them, and that they have great significance to Him. The test at the end of the age is this: Will we get that part of God's heart enough to properly represent His care and love to those who have no way of knowing it unless we demonstrate it? Will we overcome Satan's lies about God and restore His correct reputation to those who need it the most?*

How do we restore culture that reflects God's love for everyone? We must use the knowledge of God, the truth about who He is in the area of culture that we are passionate about, to show His care by bringing His solutions to every problem that tempts our hearts to believe that He doesn't care. When we know Him, we will know what He cares about. We won't care about what we think He doesn't care about. When we know what He cares about, we can access His better ways of doing everything. When things are done His way, others will know the truth about Him as the God who has made each of us in His image and given us worth and love beyond the pain we may be trapped in.

You can cooperate with God in restoring love to our culture the way God originally intended it to be. Love is action. When there's a famine, love is poured out as food. Where there is chaos, love is offered as peace. Wherever hearts believe they don't matter, love brings the truth in a practical way until the heart becomes convinced. When someone is in need and you become the solution, love has come from God through you to another one of His sons or daughters. Their perspective of God and of themselves is healed and expanded as you care about others like God does. And you care about others like He does, once you become convinced of His care for you.

<u>YOUR</u> HOPEFUL FUTURE

*As we have worked our way through the seven colors of love displayed as **strength** in **families**, **honor** in **religion**, **power** in **government**, **blessing** in **media**, **wisdom** in **education**, **riches** in **economy**, and **glory** in **art and*** *entertainment, you may be interested to understand where these came from. The last book in the Bible was written by John, who was a disciple of Jesus. Much like a prisoner of Alcatraz, John was exiled on the island of Patmos for preaching that Jesus was the Son of God. While he was there, he wrote letters that are compiled in the book of Revelation, as well as descriptions of visions he had where he was taken up to heaven.*

In one of his experiences, John was able to watch a fast-forward of history unfolding that crescendoed at the moment Jesus sacrificed Himself on the cross as a Lamb for the sin of the world. The response in heaven was profound. John says,

"They sang a new song, saying:

"You are worthy to take the scroll, and to open its seals; For You were slain, and have redeemed us to God by Your blood out of every tribe and tongue and people and nation, and have made us kings and priests to our God; and we shall reign on the earth."

"I looked, and I heard the voice of many angels around the throne, the living creatures, and the elders; and the number of them was ten thousand times ten thousand, and thousands of thousands, saying with a loud voice:

"'Worthy is the Lamb who was slain

'To receive *power* and *riches* and *wisdom*,

'And *strength* and *honor* and *glory* and *blessing!*'"

Notice they sang and celebrated the fact that heaven would reign on the earth. Heaven will truly come to earth one day in fullness, but until then, we each bring it bit by bit when we choose God and His ways.

They also shouted the seven things from each area of culture that the Lamb is worthy of receiving! People and nations will receive the love He displays as power, riches, wisdom, strength, honor, glory, and blessing and will

offer it back up to Him as worship. The One who ultimately healed your per-
spective of the heart of your Father toward you, is worthy of having His love
seen in all the ways He has poured it out. How sad it is when love is given but
not received. God doesn't need anything from us but to have sons and daugh-
ters who get His heart and receive His love. And of course when we receive
His love we can't help but give it back to Him. As sons and daughters we will
have the honored privilege of giving back to our Papa all that we received from
Him as power, riches, wisdom, strength, honor, glory, and blessing.

We spoke of each sphere of culture as having a hopeful future, and your
personal future is no less hopeful to the degree that you find Him in it. He is
there already waiting to be seen and then revealed through you in only the
way you uniquely can reveal Him. You are full of hope when you are able to
anticipate the goodness of God in all areas of your life. When you have hope
for your own life, you can easily find it for someone else and in the area of
culture you are passionate about.

RESPOND TO HIS INVITATION

We've been challenged in each chapter to invite God in. In learning about
Him, we have discovered that He is protective over our freedom to choose
Him—so much so that He waits to be invited in and will never force Himself
on us, because of His desire for authentic relationship. We have also grown
in our understanding of His heart that is quick to respond when we give
Him anything at all to work with. He is extending an invitation to us as we
invite Him in. He invites us to be ambassadors and representatives of His
image here on earth and to be conduits for His love. You may feel like you
have no real way to serve Him, but remember it's as simple as caring about
what you discover He cares about. Maybe what you're interested in seems so
non-religious that it doesn't seem to look like God. But as we've discovered,
He is not religious. He will show up anywhere and in any way that life and
freedom can be promoted.

When we look at the challenges and problems of our world on any given day, we can easily get discouraged and believe it's impossible to make a difference. In the same way that our bodies are so intricate and complicated, but the littlest of changes can bring great healing, so too is the heart of our society and the heart of man. We can have experienced profound deep wounding in many areas of life, but by one thing finally going right we can get our hope back. Great breakthrough will come and increase as we infuse individual hearts, cities, and nations with the kindness of Christ and the goodness of God.

The possibilities for impact are endless. Our Rainbow God has given us every color of His heart to paint with, so let's go cover His world with the seven colors of love.

What does Love look like coming out of YOU?

We are honored that you chose to journey through this book with us. If you would like to continue in your discovery of what God's love looks like coming out of YOU, then check out our interactive website. You can access helpful information, such as the Truth Statements we previously mentioned as a free download. We would also love to hear your story of how your perspective of God has been expanded. Simply log into www.RainbowGod.com and use the code GODISGOOD.

Johnny and Elizabeth

Rainbow God: The Seven Colors of Love Quick Reference Chart

THE SEVEN COLORS OF LOVE	ORANGE	BLUE	PURPLE
GOD as...	Papa	Redeemer	King
Area of Culture	Family	Religion	Government
Love Displayed as...	Strength	Honor	Power
The Lie Being Perpetuated About God...	We have been abandoned and rejected by God.	We have to work hard and be good in order to know God.	God does not care about us.
The Truth About God...	God has not abandoned or rejected us.	We need a redeemer in order to know God.	God does care about us.
The Lord's Prayer	Our Father, who is in heaven...	Hallowed be Your name.	Your kingdom come,

Rainbow God: The Seven Colors of Love
Quick Reference Chart

RED	INDIGO/DEEP BLUE	GREEN	YELLOW
Communicator	Teacher	Provider	Creator
Media	Education	Economy	Arts & Entertainment
Blessing	Wisdom	Riches	Glory
God doesn't have a good plan for us.	True wisdom is self dependence.	It is pointless to trust God for resources.	God doesn't want us to have fun.
God has a good plan for us.	True wisdom is dependence on God.	God enjoys providing for us and through us.	God wants us to enjoy life.
Your will be done, on earth as it is in heaven.	Give us this day our daily bread.	Forgive us our debts as we forgive our debtors.	Lead us not into temptation, but deliver us from evil, for Yours is the kingdom and the power, and the glory forever, Amen.

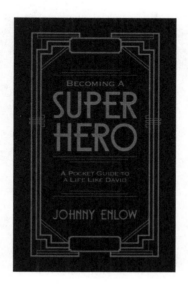

Have you ever wondered if there's more to life than you're presently experiencing?

Becoming a Superhero: A Pocket Guide to a Life Like David is an easy read, yet full of profound and unique insights into the life of David. He faced many trials and tribulations throughout his life, as many of us do. Despite his own fears and shortcomings, God used David to silence the giant that locked down an entire nation in terror. By overcoming the personal lies of rejection and insignificance that could have easily held him back, David was prepared to deal with Goliath through the supernatural power of God within him. Just like David, God wants to help you overcome all that hinders you from discovering the superhero that lives in you.

REFORMERS INFLUENCING SOCIETY EVERY DAY

RISE is the answer for radical lovers of Jesus who know they were created to change the world, but haven't known exactly what that looks like in real life. We believe God desires to partner with His sons and daughters to display His goodness in the earth and reform every broken system in every area of culture. If you're fully convinced that the real God loves the world and has solutions for every problem that exists in society, then the RISE Global Community is for you!

To find out more about RISE and upcoming events, visit our website:

www.RISE7.LA